GOODSON MUMBA

# THE MANAGER'S TOOL BOX

*Proven Techniques for Successful Leadership*

*Copyright © 2024 by Goodson Mumba*

*All rights reserved. No part of this publication may be reproduced, stored or transmitted in any form or by any means, electronic, mechanical, photocopying, recording, scanning, or otherwise without written permission from the publisher. It is illegal to copy this book, post it to a website, or distribute it by any other means without permission.*

*First edition*

*ISBN: 9798334900332*

*This book was professionally typeset on Reedsy.
Find out more at reedsy.com*

# Contents

| | | |
|---|---|---|
| *Preface* | | iv |
| *Acknowledgement* | | vi |
| *Dedication* | | vii |
| *Disclaimer* | | viii |
| 1 | Chapter One: Setting the Foundation | 1 |
| 2 | Chapter Two: Effective Communication | 12 |
| 3 | Chapter Three: Strategic Planning | 21 |
| 4 | Chapter Four: Team Building and Management | 33 |
| 5 | Chapter Five: Decision Making and Problem Solving | 43 |
| 6 | Chapter Six: Performance Management | 53 |
| 7 | Chapter Seven: Change Management | 62 |
| 8 | Chapter Eight: Emotional Intelligence and Leadership | 71 |
| 9 | Chapter Nine: Ethical Leadership | 80 |
| 10 | Chapter Ten: The Management and Prioritization | 90 |
| 11 | Chapter Eleven: Motivating and Inspiring | 100 |
| 12 | Chapter Twelve: Resolving Conflict and Negotiation | 110 |
| 13 | Chapter Thirteen: Building Resilience and Managing Stress | 120 |
| 14 | Chapter Fourteen: Leading Through Crisis | 130 |
| *About the Author* | | 139 |

# Preface

Welcome to "The Manager's Toolbox: Proven Techniques for Successful Leadership." This book is the culmination of years of experience, insights, and lessons learned in the dynamic world of leadership and management. Whether you're a seasoned executive, a budding entrepreneur, or someone aspiring to lead with impact, this book is designed to be your trusted guide on the journey to becoming an effective and successful leader.

In today's rapidly changing business landscape, the role of a manager is more important than ever. Leaders are tasked with navigating complex challenges, inspiring their teams, and driving sustainable growth in an environment characterized by uncertainty and disruption. It's a daunting task, but one that is made infinitely more manageable with the right tools, techniques, and strategies at your disposal.

"The Manager's Toolbox" is not just another leadership book filled with theoretical concepts and abstract principles. Instead, it's a practical, hands-on resource packed with actionable insights and proven techniques that you can apply directly to your day-to-day work. Each chapter is designed to address a specific aspect of leadership, from effective communication and strategic planning to team building and conflict resolution.

But more than just offering a collection of management theories, this book is grounded in real-world experience. Drawing upon decades of experience in leadership roles across various industries, the insights shared within these pages are tried, tested, and proven to deliver results. Whether it's navigating a crisis, leading through change, or inspiring others to embrace learning and growth, you'll find practical guidance and actionable strategies to help you succeed.

As you embark on your journey through "The Manager's Toolbox," I encourage you to approach each chapter with an open mind and a willingness to learn. Leadership is a journey, not a destination, and there's always room to grow and improve. So, dive in, explore the tools and techniques presented within these pages, and embrace the opportunity to become the leader you aspire to be.

Above all, remember that leadership is not just about achieving results; it's about empowering others, fostering a culture of growth and resilience, and making a positive impact in the world. With "The Manager's Toolbox" as your guide, I have no doubt that you'll be equipped to navigate the challenges of leadership with confidence, clarity, and purpose.

Here's to your success as a leader and to the journey ahead.

Warm regards,

Goodson Mumba

# Acknowledgement

I would like to eternally and gratefully acknowledge the Almighty God for the infinite intelligence from His universal mind where we draw from all that we come to know and are yet to know. May I also acknowledge and thank everyone that has played a part in my journey of life in terms of spiritual, moral, emotional and material support.

# Dedication

I extend my sincerest gratitude to my beloved wife, Edith Mumba, and our children, Angelina, Lubuto, Letticia, Lulumbi, and Butusho, for their unwavering support and understanding throughout the conception, writing, and eventual publication of this book, despite the sacrifices and challenges they endured.

# Disclaimer

This book is a work of fiction. Names, characters, businesses, places, events, and incidents are either the products of the author's imagination or used in a fictitious manner. Any resemblance to actual persons, living or dead, or actual events is purely coincidental.

# 1

# Chapter One: Setting the Foundation

Dr. Buster, a seasoned entrepreneur and author of the renowned book "The Manager's Toolbox: Proven Techniques for Successful Leadership," decides to take a step back from the day-to-day operations of his company, entrusting his two children, Wallace and Natasha, with the responsibility of running the business. Excited to prove themselves, Wallace and Natasha dive into their new roles with enthusiasm. However, they soon realize that leading a company is more challenging than they anticipated. They encounter various obstacles, from internal conflicts among employees to external market pressures. As they struggle to navigate these challenges, Wallace and Natasha find themselves on the verge of giving up. Feeling overwhelmed, they turn to their father for guidance. Instead of handing them his book, Dr. Buster shares personal anecdotes and management nuggets based on his years of experience. With their father's wisdom and encouragement, Wallace and Natasha learn valuable lessons about leadership, communication, and problem-solving. They discover that true leadership is not about following a set of rules from a book but about understanding people, adapting to change, and making tough decisions. Armed with their father's advice and a newfound sense of confidence, Wallace and Natasha tackle each challenge head-on. Through perseverance and determination, they not only overcome the obstacles facing their company but also strengthen their bond as a family.

The sun dipped low on the horizon as Dr. Buster, a figure of quiet authority, sat in his spacious office, his gaze fixed on the sprawling cityscape outside his window. For years, he had been the driving force behind the success of his company, a beacon of innovation and excellence in the business world. But now, as the twilight of his career approached, he knew it was time to pass the torch to the next generation.

With a heavy yet hopeful heart, Dr. Buster called his two children, Wallace and Natasha, into his office. They entered, their faces a mix of excitement and trepidation, knowing that their father had something important to discuss.

"Wallace, Natasha," Dr. Buster began, his voice steady yet tinged with emotion, "I've decided to take a step back from the day-to-day operations of the company. It's time for me to entrust the future of our business to you."

Wallace and Natasha exchanged a glance, their hearts swelling with pride at the trust their father was placing in them. They had always admired Dr. Buster, with his keen business acumen and unwavering commitment to excellence, and now, they were being given the opportunity to follow in his footsteps.

Excited to prove themselves, Wallace and Natasha threw themselves into their new roles with gusto. Armed with their father's guidance and the principles outlined in his renowned book, "The Manager's Toolbox," they believed they were ready

## CHAPTER ONE: SETTING THE FOUNDATION

to conquer any challenge that came their way.

But as days turned into weeks, and weeks into months, Wallace and Natasha soon discovered that leading a company was more challenging than they had ever imagined. They encountered internal conflicts among employees, external market pressures, and a myriad of unforeseen obstacles that threatened to derail their efforts.

Feeling overwhelmed and out of their depth, Wallace and Natasha found themselves on the verge of giving up. They questioned whether they were truly cut out for the responsibilities that came with leadership, whether they were living up to their father's expectations.

Sensing their doubts and fears, Dr. Buster decided it was time to offer his children more than just the tools and techniques outlined in his book. He shared personal anecdotes and management nuggets based on his years of experience, imparting wisdom that could not be found within the pages of any textbook.

With their father's guidance and encouragement, Wallace and Natasha began to see leadership in a new light. They learned that true leadership was not about following a set of rules or formulas, but about understanding people, adapting to change, and making tough decisions with integrity and conviction.

As Wallace and Natasha grappled with the weight of their newfound responsibilities, they turned to their father for guidance, hoping to glean insights that would help them navigate the complexities of leadership. Dr. Buster, sensing their uncertainty, sat them down and began to share his own experiences, offering them a deeper understanding of the role of leadership.

"Leadership isn't just about giving orders or making decisions," Dr. Buster began, his voice resonating with warmth and wisdom. "It's about inspiring others to believe in a shared vision and motivating them to work towards a common goal."

His words struck a chord with Wallace and Natasha, who realized that true leadership went beyond mere authority; it was about earning the trust and respect of those around them through actions, not just words.

Dr. Buster continued, "True leaders lead by example, demonstrating integrity, humility, and empathy in everything they do. They understand the importance of listening to others and empowering them to contribute their unique perspectives and talents."

As Wallace and Natasha listened intently, they began to see leadership in a new light. They understood that it was not about being the smartest or most powerful person in the room, but about empowering others to reach their full potential and achieve greatness together.

Dr. Buster shared stories of leaders who had inspired him throughout his career, from mentors who had guided him through difficult times to colleagues who had demonstrated unwavering dedication and commitment to their teams.

Armed with this newfound understanding, Wallace and Natasha set out to lead with humility, empathy, and authenticity, knowing that by doing so, they could inspire others to do the same. And as they embarked on this journey of self-discovery and growth, they knew that they were not just leading a company; they were building a legacy that would endure for generations to come.

As Wallace and Natasha absorbed their father's wisdom about the role of leadership, they realized that understanding their own leadership style was essential to their success. Dr. Buster, sensing their curiosity, delved into the importance of defining one's leadership style.

"Your leadership style is like a fingerprint," Dr. Buster explained, his voice carrying the weight of experience. "It's unique to you and shapes how you interact with others, make decisions, and inspire change."

Wallace and Natasha exchanged a glance, eager to learn more about how they could define their own leadership styles. Dr. Buster encouraged them to reflect on their strengths, values, and personal experiences, as these would shape their approach to leadership.

"As leaders, you have the opportunity to choose how you want to lead," Dr. Buster continued. "Whether you prefer a more hands-on approach or delegate tasks to empower your team, it's important to be authentic and true to yourself."

As they pondered Dr. Buster's words, Wallace and Natasha began to recognize their own leadership tendencies. Wallace, with his natural charisma and ability to inspire others, leaned towards a more visionary leadership style. Natasha, with her analytical mind and attention to detail, gravitated towards a more strategic and systematic approach.

Dr. Buster encouraged them to embrace their unique strengths and leverage them to create a leadership style that resonated with their team and the company's goals. He reminded them that there was no one-size-fits-all approach to leadership and that the most effective leaders were those who remained true to themselves.

Armed with this newfound insight, Wallace and Natasha set out to define their leadership styles, confident in their ability to lead with authenticity and purpose. And as they embarked on this journey of self-discovery and growth, they knew that they were not just leading a company; they were shaping the future of their family legacy.

With a newfound understanding of leadership style, Wallace and Natasha turned their attention to the next crucial aspect: establishing core values and vision for the company. Dr. Buster, sensing their determination, emphasized the importance of this step in guiding the organization towards success.

"Core values are the guiding principles that define who we are as a company," Dr. Buster explained, his voice resonating with conviction. "They serve as the foundation upon which every decision and action is based."

As Wallace and Natasha listened intently, Dr. Buster encouraged them to reflect on what truly mattered to them as leaders and what they wanted their company to stand for. Together, they brainstormed ideas and debated the merits of various values until they finally settled on a set that resonated with their shared vision.

"Integrity, innovation, and teamwork," Wallace declared, his eyes alight with passion. "These are the values that will guide us as we strive to make a positive impact on the world."

Natasha nodded in agreement, recognizing the importance of fostering a culture of trust, creativity, and collaboration within the organization. With their core values established, they turned their attention to crafting a compelling vision for the future.

"Our vision is to become a global leader in our industry, known for our commitment to excellence, innovation, and social responsibility," Natasha proclaimed, her voice ringing with confidence.

Dr. Buster smiled, proud of his children's clarity of purpose and determination to make a difference. He reminded them that a strong vision not only inspired employees but also provided a roadmap for the company's growth and success.

Armed with their core values and vision, Wallace and Natasha set out to rally their team around a common purpose, knowing that together, they could overcome any obstacle and achieve their dreams. And as they embarked on this journey of transformation and growth, they knew that they were not just building a company; they were building a legacy that would endure for generations to come.

As Wallace and Natasha delved deeper into their leadership journey, they recognized the critical importance of building trust and credibility within their organization. Dr. Buster, sensing their determination, shared insights on how trust could be cultivated and credibility earned.

"Trust is the cornerstone of effective leadership," Dr. Buster emphasized, his voice echoing with the weight of experience. "It's the foundation upon which strong relationships are built, both within the team and with external stakeholders."

Wallace and Natasha nodded in agreement, understanding that without trust, their leadership would falter, and their vision for the company would remain out of reach. Dr. Buster encouraged them to lead by example, demonstrating honesty, transparency, and integrity in everything they did.

"As leaders, your actions speak louder than words," Dr. Buster reminded them. "Be consistent in your behavior, follow through on your promises, and always prioritize the well-being of your team."

Inspired by their father's words, Wallace and Natasha set out to earn the trust of their employees and stakeholders. They engaged in open and honest communication, soliciting feedback and actively listening to the concerns and ideas of others.

They also recognized the importance of leading with empathy and compassion, taking the time to understand the needs and motivations of their team members and providing support and encouragement when needed.

As they worked tirelessly to build trust within their organization, Wallace and Natasha also focused on earning credibility in the eyes of their employees and industry peers. They leveraged their expertise and knowledge to make informed decisions and demonstrated a commitment to excellence in everything they did.

Through their actions, Wallace and Natasha began to earn the respect and admiration of those around them. Employees felt empowered and motivated to contribute their best efforts, knowing that their leaders had their best interests at heart.

Dr. Buster watched with pride as his children embraced their roles as leaders, knowing that they were well on their way to building a company culture rooted in trust, credibility, and mutual respect. And as they continued on their journey of leadership and growth, they knew that they were not just building a successful business; they were building a legacy of integrity and excellence that would endure for generations to come.

As Wallace and Natasha continued to absorb their father's wisdom, they understood that creating a positive organizational culture was paramount to the success of their company. Dr. Buster, sensing their determination, shared insights on how to foster a culture of collaboration, innovation, and positivity within the organization.

"Organizational culture is the collective personality of your company," Dr. Buster explained, his voice filled with passion.

"It's the shared values, beliefs, and behaviors that define who we are and how we work together."

Wallace and Natasha nodded in agreement, realizing that a positive culture would not only attract top talent but also inspire employees to give their best and stay committed to the company's goals. Dr. Buster encouraged them to lead by example, embodying the values they wished to instill in their team.

"As leaders, you have the power to shape the culture of your organization," Dr. Buster reminded them. "Be intentional about creating a supportive and inclusive environment where every individual feels valued and empowered to contribute."

Inspired by their father's words, Wallace and Natasha set out to cultivate a culture of positivity within their company. They fostered open communication and transparency, ensuring that employees felt heard and respected. They also promoted collaboration and teamwork, encouraging employees to share ideas and work together towards common goals.

In addition, Wallace and Natasha recognized the importance of celebrating successes and recognizing the contributions of their team members. They implemented employee recognition programs and organized team-building activities to foster camaraderie and boost morale.

As they worked tirelessly to create a positive organizational culture, Wallace and Natasha saw the impact of their efforts firsthand. Employee engagement and satisfaction soared, and productivity reached new heights as employees felt motivated and inspired to give their best.

Dr. Buster watched with pride as his children embraced their roles as leaders, knowing that they were well on their way to building a company culture that would set them apart in the industry. And as they continued on their journey of leadership and growth, they knew that they were not just building a successful business; they were building a legacy of positivity and excellence that would endure for generations to come.

As Wallace and Natasha delved deeper into their leadership journey, they realized the importance of setting SMART goals to guide their company towards success. Dr. Buster, sensing their determination, shared insights on how to create goals that were specific, measurable, achievable, relevant, and time-bound.

"SMART goals provide a clear roadmap for success," Dr. Buster explained, his voice filled with conviction. "They help you focus your efforts and track your progress, ensuring that you stay on course towards achieving your vision for the company."

Wallace and Natasha nodded in agreement, understanding that without clear goals, their vision for the company would remain just that – a vision, without direction or purpose. Dr. Buster encouraged them to be specific about what they wanted to achieve, breaking down their larger vision into smaller, actionable steps.

"Each goal should be measurable, allowing you to track your progress and celebrate your successes along the way," Dr. Buster continued. "Make sure your goals are achievable and relevant to your overall vision for the company, and set deadlines to keep you accountable and focused."

Inspired by their father's words, Wallace and Natasha set out to create SMART goals for their company. They brainstormed ideas and debated the merits of various objectives until they finally settled on a set that aligned with their core values and

## CHAPTER ONE: SETTING THE FOUNDATION

vision.

"Our first SMART goal is to increase sales by 20% within the next fiscal year," Wallace declared, his voice brimming with confidence. "We'll achieve this by launching a new marketing campaign and expanding our customer base."

Natasha nodded in agreement, recognizing the importance of setting ambitious yet attainable goals that would push the company forward. "Our second goal is to improve employee retention by 15% by implementing new training and development programs," she added. "This will help us foster a positive work environment and attract top talent."

As they finalized their SMART goals, Wallace and Natasha felt a sense of excitement and determination wash over them. They knew that with clear objectives in place, they could focus their efforts and rally their team towards achieving their shared vision for the company.

Dr. Buster watched with pride as his children embraced their roles as leaders, knowing that they were well on their way to achieving greatness. And as they continued on their journey of leadership and growth, they knew that they were not just setting goals; they were laying the foundation for a future filled with success and prosperity.

# 2

# Chapter Two: Effective Communication

As Wallace and Natasha settled into their roles as leaders, they soon realized that effective communication was the cornerstone of their success. Dr. Buster, sensing their determination, emphasized the importance of clear and concise messaging in guiding their team towards their shared goals.

"Communication is more than just words," Dr. Buster began, his voice carrying the weight of experience. "It's about conveying ideas, fostering understanding, and building trust among your team members."

Wallace and Natasha nodded in agreement, understanding that without effective communication, their vision for the company would remain out of reach. Dr. Buster encouraged them to lead by example, demonstrating active listening, empathy, and authenticity in their interactions with others.

"As leaders, you must be able to communicate your vision and expectations clearly and confidently," Dr. Buster continued. "Be open and transparent with your team, and encourage them

## CHAPTER TWO: EFFECTIVE COMMUNICATION

to share their ideas and concerns freely."

Inspired by their father's words, Wallace and Natasha set out to improve communication within their organization. They implemented regular team meetings and town hall sessions to keep everyone informed about the company's progress and goals. They also encouraged open dialogue and feedback, creating a culture where every voice was valued and heard.

In addition, Wallace and Natasha recognized the importance of tailoring their communication style to suit the needs and preferences of their team members. They adapted their approach based on individual personalities and communication styles, ensuring that everyone felt comfortable and understood.

As they worked tirelessly to improve communication within their organization, Wallace and Natasha saw the impact of their efforts firsthand. Team morale soared, and productivity reached new heights as employees felt empowered and engaged.

Dr. Buster watched with pride as his children embraced their roles as communicators, knowing that they were well on their way to building a company culture rooted in transparency, collaboration, and trust. And as they continued on their journey of leadership and growth, they knew that they were not just communicating; they were building bridges that would connect their team and propel them towards success.

In their quest to master effective communication, Wallace and Natasha recognized the profound impact of active listening and empathy in fostering understanding and building trust within their organization. Dr. Buster, sensing their determination, shared insights on how to cultivate these essential skills.

"Active listening is more than just hearing; it's about fully engaging with the speaker and seeking to understand their perspective," Dr. Buster began, his voice carrying the weight of experience. "Empathy, on the other hand, is the ability to understand and share the feelings of another."

Wallace and Natasha nodded in agreement, realizing that by listening attentively and empathizing with their team members, they could create a culture of mutual respect and support. Dr. Buster encouraged them to practice active listening in their daily interactions, setting aside their own agendas and distractions to truly focus on what others were saying.

"As leaders, you must show genuine empathy towards your team members, acknowledging their feelings and experiences," Dr. Buster continued. "By demonstrating empathy, you can build stronger connections and foster a sense of belonging within your organization."

Inspired by their father's words, Wallace and Natasha set out to hone their active listening and empathy skills. They made a conscious effort to listen with an open mind and heart, seeking to understand the perspectives and concerns of their team members without judgment or interruption.

In addition, Wallace and Natasha practiced empathy in their interactions, taking the time to put themselves in their team members' shoes and validate their emotions and experiences. They offered support and encouragement when needed, creating a safe space where everyone felt valued and understood.

As they practiced active listening and empathy, Wallace and Natasha saw the positive impact it had on their organization. Team members felt heard and appreciated, and trust among colleagues grew stronger.

Dr. Buster watched with pride as his children embraced the principles of active listening and empathy, knowing that they were well on their way to becoming compassionate and

## CHAPTER TWO: EFFECTIVE COMMUNICATION

effective leaders. And as they continued on their journey of leadership and growth, they knew that they were not just listening; they were building meaningful connections that would drive their organization towards success.

As Wallace and Natasha delved deeper into the intricacies of effective communication, they realized the importance of delivering clear and concise messages to their team members. Dr. Buster, sensing their determination, shared insights on how to craft messages that were easily understood and impactful.

"Clear and concise messaging is essential for ensuring that your team members understand your vision and goals," Dr. Buster began, his voice carrying the weight of experience. "By eliminating ambiguity and confusion, you can inspire confidence and clarity among your team."

Wallace and Natasha nodded in agreement, understanding that without clear communication, their messages could be misinterpreted or lost in translation. Dr. Buster encouraged them to be intentional about their language and delivery, ensuring that their messages were simple, direct, and to the point.

"As leaders, you must strive to communicate with clarity and precision," Dr. Buster continued. "Avoid jargon and technical language that may confuse your team members, and focus on delivering your message in a way that resonates with them."

Inspired by their father's words, Wallace and Natasha set out to refine their communication skills, paying close attention to the clarity and effectiveness of their messages. They practiced distilling complex ideas into simple, easy-to-understand language, ensuring that everyone on their team could grasp the key points.

In addition, Wallace and Natasha recognized the importance

of using multiple channels to communicate with their team members, tailoring their approach to suit different preferences and communication styles. Whether it was through face-to-face meetings, email updates, or digital platforms, they ensured that their messages reached everyone in a timely and efficient manner.

As they focused on delivering clear and concise messages, Wallace and Natasha saw the impact it had on their organization. Team members felt more informed and engaged, and productivity soared as everyone worked towards common goals with a shared understanding.

Dr. Buster watched with pride as his children embraced the principles of clear and concise messaging, knowing that they were well on their way to becoming effective communicators. And as they continued on their journey of leadership and growth, they knew that they were not just delivering messages; they were shaping the culture of their organization and paving the way for success.

As Wallace and Natasha delved deeper into their exploration of effective communication, they recognized the pivotal role of giving and receiving feedback in fostering growth and improvement within their organization. With a shared sense of determination, they sought guidance from their father on how to navigate this crucial aspect of leadership.

"Feedback is a powerful tool for personal and professional development," Dr. Buster affirmed, his voice resonating with authority. "It provides valuable insights that can help individuals and teams identify strengths, address weaknesses, and continuously improve."

Wallace and Natasha nodded in agreement, understanding that feedback was not just about pointing out mistakes but also about acknowledging achievements and encouraging growth. They realized the importance of creating a culture where feedback was welcomed and valued by all.

"As leaders, it's essential to provide feedback in a constructive and respectful manner," Dr. Buster continued. "Focus on specific behaviors and outcomes, and offer actionable suggestions for improvement."

Inspired by their father's words, Wallace and Natasha committed themselves to providing regular feedback to their team members. They scheduled one-on-one meetings and performance reviews to discuss progress, address concerns, and set goals for the future.

In addition to giving feedback, Wallace and Natasha recognized the importance of being open to receiving feedback themselves. They encouraged their team members to share their thoughts and opinions openly and honestly, knowing that constructive criticism was essential for personal and professional growth.

As they embraced the culture of feedback within their organization, Wallace and Natasha saw the positive impact it had on their team. Communication improved, morale soared, and productivity reached new heights as everyone worked together towards common goals with a shared sense of purpose.

Dr. Buster watched with pride as his children embraced the principles of giving and receiving feedback, knowing that they were well on their way to becoming effective leaders. And as they continued on their journey of leadership and growth, they knew that they were not just providing feedback; they were empowering their team to reach their full potential and achieve greatness.

As Wallace and Natasha delved deeper into the intricacies of effective communication, they encountered the inevitable challenge of navigating conflicts within their organization. With a keen awareness of the importance of fostering a harmonious workplace, they sought guidance from their father on how to effectively resolve conflicts when they arose.

Dr. Buster observed his children's determination to master this critical aspect of leadership and decided to share his insights on conflict resolution techniques. "Conflicts are inevitable in any organization," he began, his voice reflecting both empathy and experience. "But how we handle them can make all the difference in maintaining a positive and productive work environment."

Wallace and Natasha nodded in agreement, recognizing that conflicts, if left unresolved, could escalate and undermine team morale and productivity. They were eager to learn strategies for addressing conflicts constructively and preserving the cohesion of their team.

"Effective conflict resolution begins with active listening and empathy," Dr. Buster continued. "Encourage those involved to express their perspectives openly and honestly, and strive to understand their underlying interests and concerns."

Inspired by their father's guidance, Wallace and Natasha committed themselves to practicing active listening and empathy when resolving conflicts. They facilitated open and honest discussions, allowing each party to voice their grievances and perspectives without fear of judgment.

In addition to fostering understanding, Wallace and Natasha learned the importance of finding common ground and seeking mutually beneficial solutions. They encouraged compromise and collaboration, focusing on shared goals and interests rather

## CHAPTER TWO: EFFECTIVE COMMUNICATION

than individual positions.

As they implemented these conflict resolution techniques within their organization, Wallace and Natasha observed a positive shift in team dynamics. Conflicts were addressed promptly and constructively, and team members felt heard and respected.

Dr. Buster watched with pride as his children demonstrated their newfound skills in conflict resolution, knowing that they were well on their way to fostering a culture of collaboration and mutual respect within their organization. And as they continued on their journey of leadership and growth, they knew that they were not just resolving conflicts; they were building stronger relationships and paving the way for greater success.

As Wallace and Natasha delved further into their exploration of effective communication, they turned their attention to the crucial aspect of meeting management within their organization. Recognizing the significance of productive meetings in fostering collaboration and driving progress, they sought guidance from their father on how to optimize their meeting practices.

Dr. Buster observed his children's eagerness to enhance their meeting management skills and decided to share his insights on effective meeting techniques. "Meetings are a valuable opportunity to align goals, share information, and make decisions as a team," he began, his voice reflecting both wisdom and experience. "But to make the most of them, it's essential to approach them with purpose and structure."

Wallace and Natasha nodded in agreement, understanding that poorly managed meetings could waste time and energy, detracting from the organization's overall productivity. They were eager to learn strategies for conducting efficient and engaging meetings that would yield tangible results.

"Effective meeting management begins with careful planning and preparation," Dr. Buster continued. "Define clear objectives for each meeting, and create an agenda to keep discussions focused and on track."

Inspired by their father's advice, Wallace and Natasha committed themselves to meticulously planning and organizing their meetings. They identified key topics to be discussed, set specific goals for each agenda item, and allocated time slots accordingly to ensure that discussions remained focused and productive.

In addition to thorough preparation, Wallace and Natasha learned the importance of active facilitation during meetings. They encouraged participation from all attendees, solicited input from quieter team members, and kept discussions moving forward to prevent tangents and distractions.

As they implemented these effective meeting management techniques, Wallace and

Natasha noticed a positive shift in the dynamics of their meetings. Discussions were more focused, decisions were made efficiently, and attendees felt more engaged and invested in the outcomes.

Dr. Buster watched with pride as his children demonstrated their newfound skills in meeting management, knowing that they were well on their way to optimizing their organization's collaborative efforts. And as they continued on their journey of leadership and growth, they knew that they were not just conducting meetings; they were fostering a culture of efficiency and effectiveness that would propel their organization towards success.

# 3

# Chapter Three: Strategic Planning

With their foundation in effective communication firmly established, Wallace and Natasha turned their focus to the critical task of strategic planning. Recognizing the importance of setting a clear direction for their organization's future, they sought guidance from their father on how to develop a strategic plan that would guide their decisions and actions in the years to come.

Dr. Buster observed his children's determination to chart the course for their organization's success and decided to share his insights on strategic planning. "Strategic planning is the process of defining your organization's objectives and determining the actions needed to achieve them," he began, his voice resonating with authority. "It's about aligning your resources and capabilities with the opportunities and challenges of the future."

Wallace and Natasha nodded in agreement, understanding that without a clear strategic plan, their organization could drift aimlessly, without purpose or direction. They were eager to learn strategies for developing a plan that would position their organization for long-term success.

"Strategic planning begins with a thorough analysis of your organization's strengths, weaknesses, opportunities, and threats," Dr. Buster continued. "This SWOT analysis will help you identify areas of focus and prioritize your goals."

Inspired by their father's guidance, Wallace and Natasha embarked on a comprehensive SWOT analysis of their organization. They assessed their internal strengths and weaknesses, as well as external opportunities and threats in the market, gaining valuable insights into their current position and future potential.

In addition to the SWOT analysis, Wallace and Natasha learned the importance of setting clear, achievable goals and developing actionable strategies to achieve them. They identified key initiatives to pursue, allocated resources accordingly, and established metrics to track progress and measure success.

As they worked tirelessly to develop their strategic plan, Wallace and Natasha felt a sense of clarity and purpose wash over them. They could envision a future where their organization thrived, guided by a shared vision and a roadmap for success.

Dr. Buster watched with pride as his children demonstrated their commitment to strategic planning, knowing that they were well on their way to shaping the future of their organization. And as they continued on their journey of leadership and growth, they knew that they were not just planning; they were laying the foundation for a legacy of innovation and excellence that would endure for generations to come.

Observing Wallace and Natasha's fervor for strategic planning, Dr. Bruce recognized the pivotal role of a SWOT analysis in guiding their organization's future. He decided to delve deeper into the process, sharing insights on how to assess strengths, weaknesses, opportunities, and threats effectively.

Impressed by their dedication, Dr. Bruce emphasized the importance of a thorough SWOT analysis. "A SWOT analysis is like a compass, guiding you through the turbulent waters of business," he began, his voice filled with conviction. "It helps you identify what you excel at, where you need improvement, what opportunities lie ahead, and what challenges you may face."

Wallace and Natasha nodded eagerly, understanding that a comprehensive understanding of their organization's internal and external factors was essential for informed decision-making. They were determined to conduct a rigorous analysis that would provide valuable insights into their organization's position and prospects.

"Start by assessing your organization's strengths," Dr. Bruce continued. "These are the attributes, resources, and capabilities that give you a competitive advantage in the market."

Inspired by his words, Wallace and Natasha embarked on a thorough examination of their organization's strengths. They identified their talented team, innovative products, and strong brand reputation as key assets that differentiated them from competitors.

Moving on to weaknesses, Dr. Bruce encouraged Wallace and Natasha to confront their organization's vulnerabilities head-on. "Weaknesses are areas where you may be at a disadvantage compared to your competitors," he explained. "Addressing these areas is crucial for improving your overall performance."

With determination, Wallace and Natasha acknowledged areas such as outdated technology infrastructure and limited marketing resources as weaknesses that needed to be addressed to unlock their organization's full potential.

Next, Dr. Bruce guided them through the process of identifying opportunities – external factors that could positively impact their organization's growth and success. "Opportunities are like open doors waiting to be explored," he exclaimed. "By seizing them, you can propel your organization to new heights."

Wallace and Natasha brainstormed potential opportunities, including emerging markets, technological advancements, and strategic partnerships, that could fuel their organization's expansion and innovation.

Finally, Dr. Bruce cautioned them to be vigilant of threats – external factors that could pose risks to their organization's viability and competitiveness. "Threats are like storm clouds on the horizon," he warned. "By recognizing and addressing them proactively, you can mitigate their impact and safeguard your organization's future."

With renewed determination, Wallace and Natasha identified potential threats such as shifting consumer preferences, intense market competition, and economic downturns, and developed strategies to mitigate their impact.

As they concluded their SWOT analysis, Wallace and Natasha felt a sense of empowerment and clarity. Armed with valuable insights into their organization's strengths, weaknesses, opportunities, and threats, they were ready to develop a strategic plan that would propel their organization towards success.

Dr. Bruce watched with pride as his children demonstrated their commitment to strategic planning, knowing that they were well on their way to shaping the future of their organization. And as they continued on their journey of leadership and growth, he knew that they were not just analyzing; they were laying the groundwork for a future filled with promise and prosperity.

As Wallace and Natasha delved deeper into the strategic planning process, they realized the critical importance of setting clear and actionable strategic objectives for their organization. With Dr. Bruce's guidance, they understood that strategic objectives would serve as the roadmap for achieving their long-term vision and guiding their organization's growth and success.

Impressed by their determination, Dr. Bruce emphasized the significance of setting strategic objectives. "Strategic objectives are the building blocks of your strategic plan," he began, his voice filled with conviction. "They define the specific goals and targets that your organization aims to achieve within a defined timeframe."

Wallace and Natasha nodded eagerly, understanding that without clear objectives, their strategic plan would lack direction and focus. They were determined to set strategic objectives that would propel their organization towards their overarching goals and vision.

"As leaders, you must ensure that your strategic objectives are SMART – specific, measurable, achievable, relevant, and time-bound," Dr. Bruce continued. "This will ensure that they are actionable and provide a clear framework for decision-making and progress tracking."

Inspired by his words, Wallace and Natasha set out to define their strategic objectives with precision and clarity. They brainstormed key areas of focus and identified specific goals that aligned with their organization's mission and vision.

In addition to being specific and measurable, Wallace and Natasha ensured that their strategic objectives were achievable and relevant to their organization's capabilities and market opportunities. They also set realistic timelines for achieving each objective, ensuring accountability and progress tracking.

As they finalized their strategic objectives, Wallace and Natasha felt a sense of empowerment and clarity. They could envision a future where their organization thrived, guided by a set of clear and actionable goals that would drive their decision-making and actions.

Dr. Bruce watched with pride as his children demonstrated their commitment to setting strategic objectives, knowing that they were well on their way to shaping the future of their organization. And as they continued on their journey of leadership and growth, he knew that they were not just setting objectives; they were setting the stage for a future filled with success and prosperity.

Witnessing Wallace and Natasha's fervor for strategic planning, Dr. Bruce recognized the pivotal role of developing action plans to translate their strategic objectives into tangible outcomes. He decided to delve deeper into this aspect, sharing insights on how to create detailed action plans that would guide their organization's efforts and ensure success.

With admiration for their dedication, Dr. Bruce emphasized the importance of developing action plans. "Action plans are the bridge between your strategic objectives and actual implementation," he began, his voice infused with enthusiasm. "They outline the specific steps and tasks required to achieve your goals, providing a clear roadmap for execution."

Wallace and Natasha nodded eagerly, understanding that without well-defined action plans, their strategic objectives would remain mere aspirations. They were determined to create action plans that would drive their organization forward and bring their vision to life.

"As leaders, you must break down your strategic objectives into smaller, manageable tasks," Dr. Bruce continued. "Assign responsibilities, set deadlines, and establish milestones to track progress and ensure accountability."

Inspired by his words, Wallace and Natasha set out to develop detailed action plans for each of their strategic objectives. They brainstormed the necessary steps and tasks, taking into account resource allocation, timelines, and dependencies.

In addition to outlining the specific actions required, Wallace and Natasha ensured that their action plans clearly defined roles and responsibilities for each team member involved. They communicated expectations and deadlines, empowering their team members to take ownership of their tasks and contribute to the organization's success.

As they finalized their action plans, Wallace and Natasha felt a sense of purpose and clarity. They could see the path forward, illuminated by a series of actionable steps that would bring their strategic objectives to fruition.

Dr. Bruce watched with pride as his children demonstrated their commitment to developing action plans, knowing that they were well on their way to turning their vision into reality. And as they continued on their journey of leadership and growth, he knew that they were not just planning; they were laying the groundwork for a future filled with achievement and progress.

Observing Wallace and Natasha's dedication to strategic planning, Dr. Bruce acknowledged the critical importance of allocating resources effectively to support the implementation of their action plans. He decided to delve deeper into this aspect, sharing insights on how to allocate resources strategically to maximize their organization's potential for success.

With respect for their commitment, Dr. Bruce emphasized the significance of resource allocation. "Allocating resources effectively is essential for ensuring that your organization's priorities are supported and its goals are achieved," he began, his voice reflecting both wisdom and experience. "It involves identifying and assigning the right people, funds, and assets to the most critical initiatives."

Wallace and Natasha nodded thoughtfully, understanding that without proper resource allocation, even the best-laid plans could falter. They were determined to allocate their organization's resources in a way that would optimize performance and drive results.

"As leaders, you must carefully assess your organization's resources and prioritize their allocation based on the highest-impact initiatives," Dr. Bruce continued. "This may involve reallocating resources from lower-priority activities or seeking additional resources to support key strategic objectives."

Inspired by his words, Wallace and Natasha set out to evaluate their organization's resources and determine the most effective way to allocate them. They conducted a thorough assessment of their team's skills and capabilities, financial resources, and technological assets, identifying areas of strength and areas in need of additional support.

In addition to identifying resources, Wallace and Natasha ensured that their allocation decisions were guided by the organization's strategic priorities. They focused on investing resources in initiatives that aligned closely with their strategic objectives, prioritizing those that would have the greatest impact on achieving their long-term vision.

As they finalized their resource allocation plan, Wallace and Natasha felt a sense of confidence and purpose. They knew

## CHAPTER THREE: STRATEGIC PLANNING

that by allocating their organization's resources effectively, they could maximize their potential for success and drive their organization forward.

Dr. Bruce watched with pride as his children demonstrated their commitment to allocating resources effectively, knowing that they were well on their way to turning their strategic plans into reality. And as they continued on their journey of leadership and growth, he knew that they were not just allocating resources; they were investing in the future of their organization and laying the groundwork for a future filled with prosperity and achievement.

Observing Wallace and Natasha's meticulous planning efforts, Dr. Bruce stressed the importance of monitoring progress and adjusting course as essential components of effective strategic planning. He decided to delve deeper into this aspect, sharing insights on how to stay agile and responsive in the face of changing circumstances.

With appreciation for their dedication, Dr. Bruce emphasized the significance of monitoring progress. "Monitoring progress allows you to track the implementation of your action plans and measure your organization's performance against its strategic objectives," he began, his voice conveying both wisdom and urgency. "It enables you to identify areas of success and areas that may require adjustments to stay on course."

Wallace and Natasha nodded attentively, understanding that without ongoing monitoring, their strategic plans could veer off track unnoticed. They were determined to implement robust monitoring mechanisms that would keep their organization on the path to success.

"As leaders, you must establish clear metrics and key performance indicators (KPIs) to track progress towards your strategic objectives," Dr. Bruce continued. "Regularly review these metrics to assess your organization's performance and identify any deviations from your planned trajectory."

Inspired by his words, Wallace and Natasha set out to define a set of meaningful KPIs for each of their strategic objectives. They established regular review periods to assess their organization's progress, analyzing data and feedback to gauge the effectiveness of their actions.

In addition to monitoring progress, Wallace and Natasha understood the importance of being prepared to adjust course as needed. They recognized that the business landscape was dynamic and unpredictable, and that flexibility was essential for navigating unforeseen challenges and seizing new opportunities.

As they implemented their monitoring and adjustment processes, Wallace and Natasha felt a sense of empowerment and control. They knew that by staying vigilant and responsive, they could steer their organization towards its goals, even in the face of uncertainty.

Dr. Bruce watched with pride as his children demonstrated their commitment to monitoring progress and adjusting course, knowing that they were well on their way to achieving their strategic objectives. And as they continued on their journey of leadership and growth, he knew that they were not just monitoring; they were actively shaping the future of their organization, one strategic decision at a time.

Observing Wallace and Natasha's meticulous planning efforts, Dr. Bruce stressed the importance of celebrating milestones and successes as essential components of effective strategic planning. He decided to delve deeper into this aspect, sharing insights on how to foster a culture of recognition and appreciation within their organization.

With admiration for their dedication, Dr. Bruce emphasized the significance of celebrating milestones. "Celebrating milestones allows you to acknowledge and reward progress towards your strategic objectives," he began, his voice conveying both warmth and encouragement. "It energizes your team, boosts morale, and reinforces a sense of accomplishment and purpose."

Wallace and Natasha nodded enthusiastically, understanding that celebrating milestones was not just about patting themselves on the back, but about recognizing the collective effort and dedication of their team. They were determined to create a culture where achievements were celebrated and appreciated.

"As leaders, you must take the time to recognize and celebrate both big and small wins," Dr. Bruce continued. "Whether it's reaching a significant milestone, completing a challenging project, or achieving a key objective, every success deserves to be acknowledged and celebrated."

Inspired by his words, Wallace and Natasha set out to establish a system for celebrating milestones within their organization. They planned regular team meetings and events where they could publicly recognize and applaud their team members' achievements, fostering a sense of camaraderie and motivation.

In addition to celebrating milestones, Wallace and Natasha understood the importance of expressing gratitude and appreciation for their team members' contributions. They made a habit of personally thanking individuals for their hard work and dedication, acknowledging the role that each person played in the organization's success.

As they implemented their milestone celebration initiatives,

Wallace and Natasha witnessed a positive shift in their organization's culture. Team members felt valued and appreciated, and morale soared as everyone celebrated their collective achievements together.

Dr. Bruce watched with pride as his children demonstrated their commitment to celebrating milestones and successes, knowing that they were well on their way to building a strong and cohesive team. And as they continued on their journey of leadership and growth, he knew that they were not just celebrating; they were fostering a culture of recognition and appreciation that would fuel their organization's continued success.

# 4

# Chapter Four: Team Building and Management

As Wallace and Natasha embarked on their journey of leadership, they recognized the critical importance of building and managing a strong, cohesive team. With their father's guidance, they set out to cultivate a culture of collaboration and camaraderie within their organization.

Driven by their determination to lead by example, Wallace and Natasha understood that effective team building was more than just bringing people together – it was about fostering trust, respect, and mutual support among team members.

Guided by their father's wisdom, they explored innovative approaches to team building, organizing team-building activities and workshops that encouraged communication, collaboration, and problem-solving.

Through these initiatives, Wallace and Natasha witnessed the transformation of their team. Communication barriers were broken down, silos were dismantled, and bonds were forged that transcended departmental boundaries.

In addition to team building, Wallace and Natasha recognized the importance of effective team management. They embraced their roles as leaders, providing guidance, support, and mentorship to their team members, empowering them to reach their full potential.

With a clear vision and a unified team, Wallace and Natasha were poised to tackle the challenges that lay ahead. And as they continued on their journey of leadership and growth, they knew that their success depended not just on their own efforts, but on the strength and unity of their team.

Recognizing the pivotal role of hiring and onboarding in building a strong team, Wallace and Natasha delved into the exploration of best practices in recruitment and integration. They understood that bringing the right talent on board and seamlessly integrating them into the team was essential for organizational success.

Guided by their father's insights, they explored innovative approaches to hiring, focusing not only on skills and qualifications but also on cultural fit and shared values. They revamped their recruitment process, implementing rigorous screening methods and conducting thorough interviews to ensure they selected candidates who aligned with their organization's vision and ethos.

Once they identified the right candidates, Wallace and Natasha turned their attention to the onboarding process. They understood that the first few weeks were crucial for setting new hires up for success and fostering a sense of belonging within the team.

They developed comprehensive onboarding programs that provided new hires with the information, resources, and support they needed to hit the ground running. From orientation sessions to buddy systems and mentorship programs, they ensured that new team members felt welcomed, supported, and empowered from day one.

As they witnessed the positive impact of their hiring and onboarding practices, Wallace and Natasha felt a sense of pride and satisfaction. They knew that by investing in the recruitment and integration of top talent, they were laying the foundation for a strong and cohesive team that would drive their organization's success.

And as they continued on their journey of leadership and growth, they remained committed to refining and enhancing their hiring and onboarding practices, knowing that their success depended on the strength and quality of their team.

Recognizing the importance of fostering cohesion within their team, Wallace and Natasha delved into strategies for developing a strong sense of unity and collaboration among team members. They understood that team cohesion was essential for maximizing productivity, fostering innovation, and achieving shared goals.

Drawing inspiration from their father's guidance, they explored various approaches to building team cohesion, from regular team-building activities to fostering open communication and mutual respect among team members.

They organized team-building exercises that encouraged collaboration and problem-solving, fostering a sense of camaraderie and trust among team members. Through these activities, they witnessed the bonds between team members strengthen, creating a foundation of support and solidarity within the team.

In addition to team-building activities, Wallace and Natasha emphasized the importance of open communication and transparency within their team. They encouraged team members to share ideas, provide feedback, and collaborate on projects, creating a culture where everyone felt valued and respected.

As they witnessed the development of strong team cohesion, Wallace and Natasha felt a sense of pride and accomplishment. They knew that by fostering unity and collaboration within their team, they were creating a supportive environment where everyone could thrive and contribute to the organization's success.

And as they continued on their journey of leadership and growth, they remained committed to nurturing team cohesion, knowing that a strong and cohesive team was the foundation of their organization's success.

Understanding the importance of empowering their team members, Wallace and Natasha explored strategies for delegating tasks and fostering a culture of autonomy and accountability within their organization. They realized that by empowering their team members to take ownership of their work, they could unleash their full potential and drive organizational success.

Guided by their father's wisdom, they embraced the concept of delegation as a means of distributing responsibility and fostering growth within their team. They identified tasks and projects that could be delegated to team members based on their skills, interests, and expertise, empowering them to take on greater responsibility and contribute to the organization's goals.

Wallace and Natasha understood that effective delegation required clear communication and trust between leaders and team members. They communicated expectations clearly, providing guidance and support as needed, while also giving their team members the freedom to make decisions and take initiative.

As they empowered their team members to take ownership of their work, Wallace and Natasha witnessed a transformation within their organization. Team members felt empowered and motivated to contribute their best, resulting in increased productivity, innovation, and collaboration across the board.

In addition to empowering their team members, Wallace and Natasha also recognized the importance of providing opportunities for growth and development. They encouraged their team members to pursue professional development opportunities, such as training programs, workshops, and mentorship opportunities, to further enhance their skills and expertise.

As they witnessed the impact of their efforts to empower and delegate tasks, Wallace and Natasha felt a sense of pride and satisfaction. They knew that by trusting and empowering their team members, they were creating a culture of ownership, accountability, and excellence within their organization.

And as they continued on their journey of leadership and growth, they remained committed to empowering and delegating tasks, knowing that by doing so, they were unlocking the full potential of their team and driving their organization towards success.

Realizing the significance of recognizing and rewarding excellence within their team, Wallace and Natasha delved into strategies for acknowledging and appreciating outstanding contributions. They understood that by celebrating achievements and rewarding exceptional performance, they could inspire their team members to strive for excellence and foster a culture of continuous improvement.

Guided by their father's insights, they explored various approaches to recognizing and rewarding excellence, from formal recognition programs to informal expressions of appreciation. They established criteria for excellence and identified key milestones and achievements that warranted recognition.

Wallace and Natasha understood that recognition could take many forms, from public praise and awards to monetary bonuses and additional responsibilities. They tailored their approach to fit the preferences and motivations of their team members, ensuring that each individual felt valued and appreciated for their contributions.

As they implemented their recognition and reward initiatives, Wallace and Natasha witnessed a positive shift in their team's morale and motivation. Team members felt acknowledged and appreciated, leading to increased engagement, loyalty, and commitment to the organization's goals.

In addition to formal recognition programs, Wallace and Natasha also emphasized the importance of informal recognition and appreciation. They made a habit of expressing gratitude and praise to team members for their hard work and dedication, creating a culture where everyone felt valued and respected.

As they witnessed the impact of their efforts to recognize and reward excellence, Wallace and Natasha felt a sense of fulfillment and pride. They knew that by acknowledging and appreciating their team members' contributions, they were fostering a culture of excellence and empowerment within their organization.

And as they continued on their journey of leadership and growth, they remained committed to recognizing and rewarding excellence, knowing that by doing so, they were inspiring their team members to achieve their best and driving their organization towards even greater success.

As Wallace and Natasha delved deeper into team building and management, they recognized the inevitability of conflicts within their team and the importance of addressing them promptly and effectively. They understood that unresolved conflicts could undermine team cohesion and productivity, so they sought out strategies for resolving conflicts and fostering a positive work environment.

Guided by their father's wisdom, they explored various approaches to conflict resolution, from open communication and mediation to collaboration and compromise. They understood that conflicts could arise from differences in perspectives, personalities, or priorities, and that it was essential to address them constructively to maintain a harmonious team dynamic.

Wallace and Natasha prioritized creating an environment where team members felt comfortable expressing their concerns and grievances openly. They encouraged open dialogue and active listening, ensuring that all perspectives were heard and respected. By fostering a culture of transparency and empathy, they laid the groundwork for effective conflict resolution.

When conflicts did arise, Wallace and Natasha approached them with a solution-oriented mindset. They facilitated constructive conversations between the parties involved, helping them identify the root causes of the conflict and work together towards mutually beneficial resolutions. They emphasized the importance of finding common ground and seeking win-win outcomes that addressed everyone's needs and concerns.

Through their efforts, Wallace and Natasha were able to resolve conflicts swiftly and amicably, preserving team morale and cohesion. They understood that conflict resolution was not about avoiding disagreements altogether but about addressing them in a way that strengthened relationships and fostered collaboration.

In addition to addressing conflicts as they arose, Wallace and Natasha also implemented proactive measures to prevent conflicts from escalating. They provided team members with conflict resolution training and resources, equipping them with the skills and tools they needed to navigate disagreements constructively.

As they witnessed the positive impact of their efforts to resolve conflicts, Wallace and Natasha felt a sense of pride and accomplishment. They knew that by fostering a culture of open communication and collaboration, they were laying the foundation for a strong and resilient team that could overcome any challenge.

And as they continued on their journey of leadership and growth, they remained committed to addressing conflicts promptly and effectively, knowing that by doing so, they were creating an environment where everyone could thrive and contribute to the organization's success.

As Wallace and Natasha delved further into team management, they recognized the vital role of fostering a culture of collaboration within their organization. They understood that a collaborative culture was essential for harnessing the collective intelligence and creativity of their team members, driving innovation, and achieving shared goals.

Guided by their father's insights, they explored various strategies for fostering collaboration, from promoting cross-functional teamwork to creating opportunities for idea-sharing and brainstorming. They recognized that collaboration was not just about working together towards a common goal but also about creating an environment where diverse perspectives were valued and encouraged.

Wallace and Natasha prioritized creating platforms and spaces where team members could come together to share ideas, insights, and feedback. They organized regular brainstorming sessions, team meetings, and collaborative projects, providing opportunities for team members to collaborate and co-create solutions to complex challenges.

They also encouraged cross-functional collaboration, bringing together individuals from different departments and disciplines to work on projects and initiatives. By breaking down silos and fostering connections across the organization, they created a culture where innovation thrived, and ideas flourished.

In addition to promoting collaboration within their team, Wallace and Natasha also looked for opportunities to collaborate with external partners, such as vendors, customers, and industry peers. They recognized the value of diverse perspectives and expertise in driving innovation and staying ahead of the competition.

Through their efforts, Wallace and Natasha were able to foster a culture of collaboration that permeated every aspect of their organization. Team members felt empowered to contribute their ideas and expertise, knowing that their input was valued and appreciated.

As they witnessed the positive impact of their efforts to foster collaboration, Wallace and Natasha felt a sense of satisfaction and pride. They knew that by creating an environment where collaboration thrived, they were setting their organization up for success, both now and in the future.

And as they continued on their journey of leadership and

growth, they remained committed to fostering a culture of collaboration, knowing that by doing so, they were unleashing the full potential of their team and driving their organization towards even greater success.

# 5

# Chapter Five: Decision Making and Problem Solving

As Wallace and Natasha continued their journey of leadership, they recognized the critical importance of effective decision-making and problem-solving in steering their organization towards success. Armed with their father's teachings and their own determination, they set out to explore strategies for making sound decisions and tackling challenges head-on.

Driven by their commitment to lead with confidence and clarity, Wallace and Natasha delved into the art and science of decision-making. They understood that decision-making was not just about choosing between options but about evaluating risks, weighing alternatives, and considering the long-term implications of their choices.

Drawing inspiration from their father's wisdom, they explored various decision-making frameworks and methodologies, from the rational decision-making model to intuitive and collaborative approaches. They recognized that different situations called for different decision-making techniques and adapted their approach accordingly.

Wallace and Natasha also understood that effective decision-making required a combination of analysis and intuition. They relied on data and evidence to inform their decisions, but they also trusted their instincts and intuition when faced with uncertainty or ambiguity.

In addition to decision-making, Wallace and Natasha focused on developing their problem-solving skills. They understood that problems were inevitable in business and that their ability to solve them effectively could make or break their organization's success.

They embraced a systematic approach to problem-solving, breaking down complex issues into manageable components and brainstorming creative solutions. They encouraged collaboration and diverse perspectives, recognizing that innovation often stemmed from a diversity of thought.

Through their efforts, Wallace and Natasha were able to make informed decisions and solve problems effectively, guiding their organization through challenges and towards opportunities. They understood that decision-making and problem-solving were not just skills; they were essential tools for navigating the ever-changing landscape of business.

And as they continued on their journey of leadership and growth, they remained committed to honing their decision-making and problem-solving abilities, knowing that by doing so, they were equipping themselves with the tools they needed to lead their organization towards success.

As Wallace and Natasha delved deeper into decision-making, they understood the importance of analyzing options and risks before making any critical choices. They realized that a thorough evaluation of potential outcomes and associated risks was essential for making informed decisions and minimizing potential pitfalls.

Guided by their father's teachings, they explored various methods for analyzing options and risks. They recognized the value of gathering relevant data, conducting thorough research, and considering multiple perspectives before weighing their options.

Wallace and Natasha embraced a systematic approach to option analysis, breaking down complex decisions into smaller components and evaluating the pros and cons of each alternative. They sought input from stakeholders, soliciting their insights and perspectives to ensure a comprehensive evaluation of all available options.

In addition to analyzing options, Wallace and Natasha prioritized assessing risks associated with each decision. They understood that every choice came with its own set of potential risks, ranging from financial implications to operational challenges and market uncertainties.

They conducted risk assessments to identify potential obstacles and develop mitigation strategies to address them. They weighed the likelihood and impact of each risk, prioritizing their responses based on the severity of the potential consequences.

Through their efforts, Wallace and Natasha were able to make informed decisions that balanced potential rewards with associated risks. They understood that while risk-taking was inherent in business, strategic risk management was essential for safeguarding their organization's future.

As they continued to refine their skills in analyzing options and risks, Wallace and Natasha felt a sense of confidence and assurance in their decision-making abilities. They knew that by taking a systematic approach to evaluating options and mitigating risks, they were setting their organization up for success in an ever-changing business landscape.

And as they continued on their journey of leadership and growth, they remained committed to honing their skills in option analysis and risk assessment, knowing that by doing so, they were positioning themselves to navigate challenges and seize opportunities with clarity and purpose.

As Wallace and Natasha continued their exploration of effective decision-making, they recognized the power of using data and insights to inform their choices. They understood that in today's data-driven world, access to accurate information and meaningful insights was crucial for making informed decisions that would drive their organization forward.

Inspired by their father's teachings, they delved into the world of data analytics and business intelligence, seeking to leverage data to gain a deeper understanding of their organization's performance, market trends, and customer behavior.

Wallace and Natasha embraced technology and analytics tools, gathering data from various sources and analyzing it to uncover valuable insights. They examined key performance indicators, market research reports, and customer feedback to identify patterns, trends, and opportunities.

In addition to quantitative data, Wallace and Natasha also recognized the value of qualitative insights. They conducted interviews, focus groups, and surveys to gather qualitative feedback from employees, customers, and stakeholders, providing them with a more holistic understanding of the factors influencing their decisions.

Armed with data and insights, Wallace and Natasha were able

to make informed decisions that were grounded in evidence and driven by data. They understood that while intuition and experience were valuable, data provided them with objective information that could guide their choices and mitigate risks.

Through their efforts, Wallace and Natasha were able to uncover new opportunities, identify potential challenges, and make strategic decisions that propelled their organization forward. They realized that by harnessing the power of data and insights, they could make smarter, more informed decisions that would drive their organization's success in an increasingly competitive business environment.

And as they continued on their journey of leadership and growth, they remained committed to leveraging data and insights to inform their decisions, knowing that by doing so, they were equipping themselves with the knowledge and understanding they needed to lead their organization towards success.

As Wallace and Natasha delved deeper into the realm of decision-making, they recognized the importance of encouraging creativity and fostering innovation within their organization. They understood that by nurturing a culture of creativity and innovation, they could unlock new opportunities, drive growth, and stay ahead of the competition.

Inspired by their father's teachings, they explored various strategies for fostering creativity and innovation. They recognized that innovation was not just about generating new ideas but also about creating an environment where ideas could flourish and evolve.

Wallace and Natasha encouraged their team members to think outside the box and challenge the status quo. They promoted brainstorming sessions, idea-sharing platforms, and innovation challenges, providing opportunities for team members to explore new concepts and experiment with novel approaches.

In addition to encouraging creativity, Wallace and Natasha also recognized the importance of creating a supportive environment where innovation could thrive. They celebrated experimentation and risk-taking, acknowledging that not every idea would be successful but that every failure was an opportunity to learn and grow.

They encouraged cross-functional collaboration and diversity of thought, recognizing that innovation often stemmed from the intersection of different perspectives and disciplines. They empowered their team members to take ownership of their ideas and pursue innovative solutions to the challenges they faced.

Through their efforts, Wallace and Natasha were able to foster a culture of creativity and innovation within their organization. Team members felt empowered to share their ideas and explore new possibilities, leading to a steady stream of innovative solutions and breakthroughs.

As they witnessed the impact of their efforts to encourage creativity and innovation, Wallace and Natasha felt a sense of excitement and possibility. They knew that by fostering a culture where creativity and innovation were valued and encouraged, they were laying the groundwork for a future filled with growth and success.

And as they continued on their journey of leadership and growth, they remained committed to nurturing creativity and innovation within their organization, knowing that by doing so, they were positioning themselves to thrive in an ever-changing business landscape.

## CHAPTER FIVE: DECISION MAKING AND PROBLEM SOLVING

As Wallace and Natasha delved further into the realm of decision-making, they acknowledged the significance of leveraging critical thinking skills to navigate complex challenges and make informed choices. They understood that critical thinking was essential for evaluating information, analyzing situations, and making sound judgments in a rapidly evolving business environment.

Inspired by their father's insights, they explored various strategies for honing their critical thinking skills. They recognized the importance of questioning assumptions, examining evidence, and considering multiple perspectives before arriving at conclusions.

Wallace and Natasha embraced a systematic approach to critical thinking, breaking down complex problems into smaller components and applying logical reasoning to assess each aspect. They sought to identify underlying patterns and connections, enabling them to make more informed decisions based on a deeper understanding of the issues at hand.

In addition to analytical thinking, Wallace and Natasha also valued creative thinking as a complementary skill in the decision-making process. They encouraged brainstorming sessions, idea generation exercises, and lateral thinking techniques to explore unconventional solutions and uncover hidden opportunities.

Armed with their critical thinking skills, Wallace and Natasha were able to approach decision-making with clarity and confidence. They understood that critical thinking was not just about finding the right answers but also about asking the right questions and challenging assumptions to arrive at the best possible outcomes.

Through their efforts, Wallace and Natasha were able to

navigate complex challenges and make informed decisions that propelled their organization forward. They realized that by leveraging their critical thinking skills, they could overcome obstacles, seize opportunities, and achieve their goals with greater precision and effectiveness.

And as they continued on their journey of leadership and growth, they remained committed to honing their critical thinking skills, knowing that by doing so, they were equipping themselves with the tools they needed to lead their organization towards success in an increasingly complex and dynamic business landscape.

As Wallace and Natasha advanced in their exploration of decision-making, they encountered the inevitable need to make tough calls with confidence. They understood that leadership often required difficult decisions that carried significant consequences, and they were prepared to face these challenges head-on.

Inspired by their father's guidance, they delved into strategies for making tough calls with confidence. They recognized the importance of balancing intuition with analysis, drawing on both their gut instincts and reasoned judgment to navigate complex decisions.

Wallace and Natasha understood that making tough calls required courage and conviction. They embraced uncertainty and ambiguity, trusting in their abilities to weigh the available information and make the best possible decisions given the circumstances.

In addition to confidence in their own abilities, Wallace and Natasha also recognized the importance of seeking input from others when faced with tough decisions. They consulted with trusted advisors, sought diverse perspectives, and solicited feedback from stakeholders to gain a more comprehensive understanding of the situation and its implications.

Armed with their resolve and determination, Wallace and Natasha were able to make tough calls with confidence. They understood that while not every decision would be easy or popular, it was their responsibility as leaders to make the choices that were in the best interests of their organization and its stakeholders.

Through their efforts, Wallace and Natasha gained a deeper sense of self-assurance and resilience. They knew that by facing tough decisions head-on and standing by their choices with confidence, they were demonstrating their commitment to leading with integrity and conviction.

And as they continued on their journey of leadership and growth, they remained steadfast in their resolve to make tough calls with confidence, knowing that by doing so, they were charting a course for their organization's success in the face of uncertainty and adversity.

As Wallace and Natasha delved deeper into the intricacies of decision-making, they recognized the inevitability of mistakes and the importance of learning from them to refine their approach and iterate solutions. They understood that setbacks were an inherent part of leadership and that embracing failure as an opportunity for growth was essential for long-term success.

Drawing upon their father's wisdom, they explored strategies for learning from mistakes and iterating solutions. They acknowledged that mistakes were not failures but rather valuable learning experiences that provided insights into what worked and what didn't.

Wallace and Natasha fostered a culture of psychological

safety within their organization, where team members felt empowered to take risks and experiment with new ideas without fear of judgment or reprisal. They encouraged open communication and transparency, creating an environment where mistakes could be openly acknowledged and analyzed.

In addition to fostering a culture of learning, Wallace and Natasha also recognized the importance of reflection and self-awareness in the process of iterating solutions. They took the time to reflect on their decisions and actions, seeking to understand the root causes of their mistakes and identify opportunities for improvement.

Armed with their newfound insights, Wallace and Natasha were able to iterate their solutions and refine their approach to decision-making. They understood that success was not about avoiding mistakes altogether but about learning from them and continuously improving over time.

Through their efforts, Wallace and Natasha demonstrated resilience and adaptability in the face of adversity. They embraced failure as a natural part of the learning process and used it as fuel to drive their organization forward.

And as they continued on their journey of leadership and growth, they remained committed to learning from their mistakes and iterating their solutions, knowing that by doing so, they were building a foundation for long-term success and resilience in an ever-changing business landscape.

# 6

# Chapter Six: Performance Management

As Wallace and Natasha progressed in their journey of leadership, they recognized the importance of effective performance management in driving their organization towards excellence. They understood that performance management was not just about evaluating individual performance but also about aligning goals, providing feedback, and fostering a culture of continuous improvement.

Guided by their father's teachings, they delved into strategies for cultivating excellence through performance management. They recognized the importance of setting clear expectations and goals, providing regular feedback and coaching, and recognizing and rewarding achievements.

Wallace and Natasha prioritized setting clear goals and expectations for their team members, ensuring that everyone understood their roles and responsibilities and how they contributed to the organization's overall objectives. They believed that clarity of purpose was essential for motivating and empowering their team members to perform at their best.

In addition to goal-setting, Wallace and Natasha also emphasized the importance of providing regular feedback and coaching to their team members. They understood that feedback was a powerful tool for growth and development, and they made it a priority to provide timely and constructive feedback to help their team members improve and grow.

They also recognized the importance of recognizing and rewarding achievements. They celebrated milestones and successes, acknowledging the hard work and dedication of their team members and motivating them to continue striving for excellence.

Through their efforts, Wallace and Natasha were able to cultivate a culture of excellence within their organization. Team members felt supported, valued, and empowered to perform at their best, driving the organization towards its goals with passion and dedication.

As they continued on their journey of leadership and growth, Wallace and Natasha remained committed to fostering excellence through performance management, knowing that by doing so, they were setting their organization up for success in the long run.

As Wallace and Natasha delved further into performance management, they understood the critical importance of setting clear expectations and standards for their team members. They recognized that clarity in expectations was essential for aligning individual efforts with organizational goals and fostering accountability and productivity.

Inspired by their father's teachings, they sought out strategies for setting clear expectations and standards. They understood that communication was key and made it a priority to articulate expectations clearly and explicitly to their team members.

## CHAPTER SIX: PERFORMANCE MANAGEMENT

Wallace and Natasha established clear performance metrics and standards for each role within their organization, outlining specific goals, objectives, and key performance indicators. They ensured that team members understood what was expected of them and how their performance would be evaluated.

In addition to setting expectations, Wallace and Natasha also emphasized the importance of providing context and rationale behind their expectations. They explained the "why" behind the "what," helping team members understand the importance of their roles and how their contributions contributed to the organization's overall success.

Through their efforts, Wallace and Natasha were able to create a culture of clarity and accountability within their organization. Team members knew exactly what was expected of them and were empowered to take ownership of their roles and responsibilities.

As they continued to refine their approach to setting expectations and standards, Wallace and Natasha felt a sense of confidence and assurance in their ability to lead their team towards excellence. They knew that by establishing clear expectations and standards, they were laying the foundation for a high-performing and cohesive team that could achieve extraordinary results.

As Wallace and Natasha ventured deeper into performance management, they recognized the pivotal role of providing feedback and coaching in nurturing their team's growth and development. They understood that feedback was a powerful tool for guiding their team members towards improvement and empowering them to reach their full potential.

Drawing from their father's wisdom, they explored various approaches to providing feedback and coaching. They realized that effective feedback was not just about pointing out areas for improvement but also about acknowledging strengths and providing guidance for growth.

Wallace and Natasha prioritized regular check-ins and one-on-one meetings with their team members, providing them with opportunities to discuss their progress, receive feedback, and address any challenges or concerns. They adopted a coaching mindset, focusing on helping their team members identify their strengths and areas for development and providing support and guidance to help them overcome obstacles and achieve their goals.

In addition to formal feedback sessions, Wallace and Natasha also embraced informal feedback opportunities, providing real-time feedback and recognition to their team members as situations arose. They understood the importance of timely feedback in reinforcing positive behaviors and addressing issues before they escalated.

Through their efforts, Wallace and Natasha were able to create a culture of continuous feedback and coaching within their organization. Team members felt supported and valued, knowing that their leaders were invested in their growth and development.

As they continued to refine their approach to providing feedback and coaching, Wallace and Natasha felt a sense of fulfillment and satisfaction in seeing their team members thrive. They knew that by providing constructive feedback and coaching, they were empowering their team members to become the best versions of themselves and driving their organization towards success.

As Wallace and Natasha delved deeper into performance management, they recognized the importance of conducting performance reviews fairly and impartially. They understood that performance reviews were a critical opportunity to provide feedback, assess progress, and align individual goals with organizational objectives.

Inspired by their father's teachings, they sought out strategies for conducting performance reviews fairly and objectively. They recognized the importance of transparency and consistency in the review process, ensuring that all team members were evaluated based on clear and consistent criteria.

Wallace and Natasha established a formal performance review process, outlining specific performance metrics and evaluation criteria for each role within their organization. They ensured that performance reviews were conducted at regular intervals and that team members received timely feedback on their performance throughout the year.

In addition to setting clear expectations, Wallace and Natasha also emphasized the importance of fairness and objectivity in the review process. They made it a priority to base performance evaluations on objective data and evidence, rather than subjective opinions or biases.

They also encouraged open communication and dialogue during performance reviews, providing team members with the opportunity to share their perspectives and feedback on their performance. They believed that a collaborative approach to performance reviews fostered trust and accountability within their organization.

Through their efforts, Wallace and Natasha were able to conduct performance reviews that were perceived as fair and equitable by their team members. Team members felt valued and respected, knowing that their performance was evaluated fairly and objectively.

As they continued to refine their approach to performance reviews, Wallace and Natasha felt a sense of pride in their ability to foster a culture of fairness and transparency within their organization. They knew that by conducting performance reviews fairly, they were empowering their team members to grow and succeed, driving their organization towards excellence.

As Wallace and Natasha delved deeper into performance management, they acknowledged the importance of addressing performance issues promptly and effectively. They understood that timely intervention was essential for maintaining high standards of performance and ensuring the success of their organization.

Guided by their father's teachings, they explored strategies for addressing performance issues promptly and constructively. They recognized that ignoring performance issues could have detrimental effects on team morale and productivity, and they were committed to taking proactive steps to address them.

Wallace and Natasha made it a priority to provide timely feedback to team members who were struggling to meet performance expectations. They approached these conversations with empathy and compassion, seeking to understand the underlying reasons for the performance issues and offering support and guidance to help team members improve.

In addition to providing feedback, Wallace and Natasha also implemented corrective action plans when necessary to address persistent performance issues. They worked closely with team members to establish clear goals and expectations for improvement, providing them with the resources and support they needed to succeed.

Through their efforts, Wallace and Natasha were able to

address performance issues promptly and effectively, maintaining a high standard of performance within their organization. Team members felt supported and empowered to overcome challenges and improve their performance, knowing that their leaders were invested in their success.

As they continued to refine their approach to addressing performance issues, Wallace and Natasha felt a sense of satisfaction in seeing their team members thrive. They knew that by addressing performance issues promptly and constructively, they were fostering a culture of accountability and continuous improvement within their organization, driving it towards greater success and achievement.

As Wallace and Natasha delved deeper into performance management, they recognized the importance of developing individual growth plans for their team members. They understood that supporting the professional development of their employees was essential for fostering a culture of continuous learning and growth within their organization.

Inspired by their father's teachings, they sought out strategies for developing individual growth plans that were tailored to the unique strengths, interests, and career aspirations of each team member. They recognized that one-size-fits-all approaches were not effective and that personalized development plans were key to unlocking the full potential of their team.

Wallace and Natasha engaged in regular conversations with their team members to understand their career goals and aspirations. They conducted skills assessments and performance evaluations to identify areas for development and growth opportunities.

Using this information, Wallace and Natasha worked collaboratively with each team member to create individual growth plans that outlined specific goals, milestones, and action steps for achieving their professional development objectives. They ensured that these plans were aligned with the overall goals and objectives of the organization, providing a clear roadmap for career advancement and growth.

In addition to setting goals and action steps, Wallace and Natasha also provided ongoing support and mentorship to their team members as they worked towards their development objectives. They offered guidance, resources, and opportunities for learning and skill-building, empowering their team members to take ownership of their professional growth.

Through their efforts, Wallace and Natasha were able to develop individual growth plans that were meaningful and impactful for their team members. Team members felt valued and supported, knowing that their leaders were invested in their development and success.

As they continued to refine their approach to developing individual growth plans, Wallace and Natasha felt a sense of fulfillment in seeing their team members grow and thrive. They knew that by investing in the professional development of their employees, they were not only building a stronger, more capable team but also laying the foundation for the long-term success and sustainability of their organization.

As Wallace and Natasha delved deeper into performance management, they understood the importance of inspiring motivation and accountability within their team. They recognized that motivated and accountable employees were essential for driving the organization towards its goals and maintaining a high level of performance.

Taking cues from their father's teachings, they explored strategies for inspiring motivation and fostering accountability among their team members. They knew that motivation stemmed from a sense of purpose and ownership, so they made it a priority to communicate the organization's vision and goals clearly and passionately.

Wallace and Natasha also understood the importance of creating a culture of accountability where team members felt responsible for their actions and outcomes. They set clear expectations and held themselves and their team members to high standards of performance, ensuring that everyone understood their role in achieving the organization's objectives.

In addition to setting expectations, Wallace and Natasha also recognized the importance of providing recognition and rewards for achievements. They celebrated successes, both big and small, and acknowledged the hard work and dedication of their team members, motivating them to continue striving for excellence.

Through their efforts, Wallace and Natasha were able to inspire motivation and foster accountability within their team. Team members felt empowered and engaged, knowing that their contributions were valued and that they had a stake in the organization's success.

As they continued to refine their approach to inspiring motivation and accountability, Wallace and Natasha felt a sense of pride in seeing their team members perform at their best. They knew that by creating a culture of motivation and accountability, they were setting their organization up for long-term success and sustainability.

# 7

# Chapter Seven: Change Management

As Wallace and Natasha delved into the complexities of leadership, they encountered the inevitable reality of change within their organization. They understood that change was a constant in the business world and that their ability to navigate and manage it would be crucial for the success and growth of their company.

Guided by their father's wisdom, they embarked on a journey to understand the principles of change management. They recognized that successful change management required careful planning, effective communication, and strong leadership.

Wallace and Natasha understood that change could be met with resistance, so they made it a priority to communicate openly and transparently with their team members about the reasons behind the change and the anticipated benefits. They emphasized the importance of involving their team members in the change process, soliciting their input and feedback, and addressing any concerns or apprehensions they may have.

In addition to communication, Wallace and Natasha also focused on providing support and resources to their team members to help them adapt to the changes. They offered training, coaching, and mentorship opportunities to ensure that everyone had the skills and knowledge they needed to succeed in the new environment.

Through their efforts, Wallace and Natasha were able to navigate change successfully within their organization. Team members felt empowered and engaged, knowing that their leaders were committed to their success and well-being.

As they continued to lead their organization through change, Wallace and Natasha remained steadfast in their commitment to embracing change as an opportunity for growth and innovation. They knew that by fostering a culture of adaptability and resilience, they were positioning their organization for long-term success in an ever-changing business landscape.

As Wallace and Natasha ventured deeper into the realm of change management, they recognized the critical importance of understanding the need for change within their organization. They understood that change was not merely a disruption but a necessary evolution to keep their company relevant and competitive in a dynamic market landscape.

Drawing insights from their father's teachings, they sought to uncover the underlying drivers and motivations behind the need for change. They conducted thorough analyses of market trends, customer preferences, and internal processes to identify areas where adaptation and transformation were imperative for sustained success.

Wallace and Natasha engaged in candid discussions with their team members to convey the rationale behind the proposed changes and to highlight the potential benefits and opportunities that would arise from embracing them. They emphasized the significance of staying ahead of industry shifts and seizing opportunities for innovation and growth.

In addition to understanding the external factors driving change, Wallace and Natasha also recognized the importance of introspection and self-assessment within their organization. They encouraged a culture of continuous improvement and self-reflection, challenging their team members to critically evaluate existing practices and processes and identify areas where change was needed to drive performance and efficiency.

Through their efforts, Wallace and Natasha fostered a deep understanding of the need for change within their organization. Team members embraced the importance of adaptation and evolution, recognizing change not as a threat but as a pathway to greater success and sustainability.

As they continued to lead their organization through the journey of change, Wallace and Natasha remained committed to fostering a culture of innovation and agility. They knew that by understanding the need for change and embracing it wholeheartedly, they were paving the way for a brighter and more prosperous future for their company.

As Wallace and Natasha delved deeper into change management, they recognized the paramount importance of communicating change effectively within their organization. They understood that clear and transparent communication was the cornerstone of successful change implementation, ensuring that everyone understood the reasons behind the change and felt empowered to navigate it.

Guided by their father's teachings, they embarked on a mission to communicate change with clarity, empathy, and authenticity. They knew that effective communication required more than just conveying information; it involved engaging with their team members on an emotional level, addressing their concerns, and inspiring confidence in the change process.

Wallace and Natasha adopted a multi-faceted approach to communicating change, utilizing various channels and platforms to reach their team members. They held town hall meetings, sent out regular updates via email, and leveraged digital communication tools to ensure that everyone had access to timely and relevant information about the changes ahead.

In addition to formal communication channels, Wallace and Natasha also emphasized the importance of one-on-one conversations and small group discussions. They made themselves accessible to their team members, inviting questions and feedback and providing personalized support to those who needed it.

Through their efforts, Wallace and Natasha were able to communicate change effectively within their organization. Team members felt informed and engaged, knowing that their leaders were committed to keeping them in the loop and involving them in the change process.

As they continued to navigate the complexities of change management, Wallace and Natasha remained steadfast in their commitment to transparent and empathetic communication. They knew that by communicating change effectively, they were not only facilitating smoother transitions but also building trust and resilience within their organization.

As Wallace and Natasha journeyed further into the realm of change management, they encountered the inevitable challenges of addressing resistance and overcoming obstacles within their organization. They understood that change often met with skepticism and apprehension, but they were determined to navigate these challenges with resilience and determination.

Guided by their father's wisdom, they embraced a proactive approach to addressing resistance, recognizing that understanding the root causes of resistance was crucial to overcoming it. They engaged in open dialogue with team members, actively listening to their concerns and perspectives, and seeking to address them with empathy and understanding.

Wallace and Natasha also recognized that overcoming obstacles required persistence and perseverance. They understood that change was not always easy and that obstacles were inevitable along the way. But they remained steadfast in their commitment to their vision, rallying their team members around common goals and inspiring them to overcome challenges together.

In addition to addressing resistance, Wallace and Natasha focused on building resilience within their organization. They encouraged a culture of adaptability and innovation, empowering their team members to embrace change as an opportunity for growth and development.

Through their efforts, Wallace and Natasha were able to overcome obstacles and address resistance within their organization. Team members felt supported and empowered, knowing that their leaders were committed to their success and well-being.

As they continued to lead their organization through change, Wallace and Natasha remained vigilant in their efforts to address resistance and overcome obstacles. They knew that by fostering resilience and determination within their organization, they were paving the way for a brighter and more prosperous future for their company.

As Wallace and Natasha delved deeper into change management, they recognized the importance of leading by example during transitions within their organization. They understood that their actions spoke louder than words, and that their behavior would set the tone for how others approached change.

Guided by their father's teachings, they embraced the role of role models, demonstrating resilience, adaptability, and positivity in the face of change. They remained calm and composed, even in the midst of uncertainty, inspiring confidence and trust among their team members.

Wallace and Natasha understood that leading by example meant more than just talking about change; it meant embodying the values and principles they wished to see in their organization. They remained committed to their vision, staying true to their values and principles even when faced with challenges and setbacks.

In addition to leading by example, Wallace and Natasha also prioritized empathy and compassion in their leadership approach. They understood that change could be difficult and unsettling for some team members, and they made it a priority to offer support and encouragement to those who needed it.

Through their actions, Wallace and Natasha were able to lead by example during transitions within their organization. Team members looked to them for guidance and inspiration, knowing that they could count on their leaders to navigate change with integrity and grace.

As they continued to lead their organization through transitions, Wallace and Natasha remained steadfast in their commitment to leading by example. They knew that by demonstrating resilience, adaptability, and empathy, they were not only guiding their organization through change but also fostering a culture of trust, collaboration, and growth.

As Wallace and Natasha delved deeper into change management, they recognized the importance of leading by example during transitions within their organization. They understood that their actions spoke louder than words, and that their behavior would set the tone for how others approached change.

Guided by their father's teachings, they embraced the role of role models, demonstrating resilience, adaptability, and positivity in the face of change. They remained calm and composed, even in the midst of uncertainty, inspiring confidence and trust among their team members.

Wallace and Natasha understood that leading by example meant more than just talking about change; it meant embodying the values and principles they wished to see in their organization. They remained committed to their vision, staying true to their values and principles even when faced with challenges and setbacks.

In addition to leading by example, Wallace and Natasha also prioritized empathy and compassion in their leadership approach. They understood that change could be difficult and unsettling for some team members, and they made it a priority to offer support and encouragement to those who needed it.

Through their actions, Wallace and Natasha were able to lead by example during transitions within their organization. Team members looked to them for guidance and inspiration, knowing that they could count on their leaders to navigate change with integrity and grace.

As they continued to lead their organization through transitions, Wallace and Natasha remained steadfast in their commitment to leading by example. They knew that by demonstrating resilience, adaptability, and empathy, they were not only guiding their organization through change but also fostering a culture of trust, collaboration, and growth.

## CHAPTER SEVEN: CHANGE MANAGEMENT

As Wallace and Natasha delved deeper into the intricacies of change management, they grasped the significance of sustaining change through continuous improvement within their organization. They recognized that change was not a one-time event but an ongoing process that required vigilance and dedication to maintain momentum and drive lasting results.

Guided by their father's sagacity, they embraced the notion of continuous improvement as a means to sustain change and drive organizational growth. They understood that complacency was the enemy of progress and that constant innovation and refinement were essential for staying ahead in a competitive business landscape.

Wallace and Natasha committed themselves to fostering a culture of continuous improvement within their organization, where every team member was encouraged to challenge the status quo, experiment with new ideas, and seek out opportunities for enhancement. They recognized that sustained change required the collective effort and engagement of all team members, from top leadership to frontline employees.

In addition to promoting a culture of continuous improvement, Wallace and Natasha also implemented mechanisms and processes to support ongoing change initiatives. They established regular review cycles and performance metrics to monitor the effectiveness of change efforts and identify areas for refinement and enhancement.

Through their unwavering commitment to continuous improvement, Wallace and Natasha were able to sustain change within their organization and drive ongoing progress and innovation. Team members felt empowered and motivated to contribute to the organization's success, knowing that their efforts were part of a larger journey towards excellence.

As they continued to lead their organization through change, Wallace and Natasha remained vigilant in their pursuit of continuous improvement. They knew that by fostering a culture of innovation and adaptability, they were laying the foundation for sustained success and resilience in the face of future challenges.

# 8

# Chapter Eight: Emotional Intelligence and Leadership

As Wallace and Natasha progressed in their leadership journey, they encountered the profound impact of emotional intelligence on effective leadership within their organization. They understood that leadership wasn't just about making decisions or setting goals; it was also about understanding and managing emotions, both their own and those of their team members.

Guided by their father's wisdom, they embarked on a quest to develop their emotional intelligence and cultivate a leadership style that prioritized empathy, self-awareness, and interpersonal relationships. They recognized that by honing their emotional intelligence skills, they could build stronger connections with their team members, inspire trust, and foster a positive work environment.

Wallace and Natasha delved into the various components of emotional intelligence, from self-awareness and self-regulation to empathy and social skills. They engaged in introspection and reflection, seeking to better understand their own emotions and how they influenced their behavior and decision-making as leaders.

In addition to developing their own emotional intelligence, Wallace and Natasha also focused on nurturing emotional intelligence within their team. They encouraged open communication and vulnerability, creating a safe space for team members to express their emotions and concerns without fear of judgment or reprisal.

Through their efforts, Wallace and Natasha were able to cultivate a culture of emotional intelligence within their organization. Team members felt valued and supported, knowing that their leaders were attuned to their emotions and invested in their well-being.

As they continued to lead their organization with heart, Wallace and Natasha remained committed to further developing their emotional intelligence skills. They knew that by leading with empathy and understanding, they were not only driving performance and productivity but also creating a workplace where people felt valued, respected, and empowered to thrive.

As Wallace and Natasha delved deeper into the exploration of emotional intelligence, they understood the profound impact of self-awareness and self-regulation on effective leadership. They recognized that self-awareness, the ability to recognize and understand one's own emotions, thoughts, and behaviors, was the foundation upon which strong leadership was built.

Guided by their father's wisdom, they embarked on a journey of self-discovery, seeking to gain deeper insights into their own emotions, strengths, and weaknesses. They engaged in introspective practices such as journaling, meditation, and self-reflection, allowing them to uncover hidden patterns and biases that influenced their leadership style.

In addition to self-awareness, Wallace and Natasha recognized the importance of self-regulation, the ability to manage and control one's emotions and impulses. They understood that effective leaders were able to remain calm and composed in the face of adversity, making rational decisions based on logic and reason rather than being driven by emotion.

Wallace and Natasha practiced self-regulation through techniques such as deep breathing, mindfulness, and positive self-talk. They learned to pause and reflect before reacting to challenging situations, allowing themselves the space to choose a response that was aligned with their values and goals as leaders.

Through their efforts to develop self-awareness and self-regulation, Wallace and Natasha became more effective and empathetic leaders. They were better able to understand the impact of their actions on others and to regulate their emotions in order to maintain a positive and productive work environment.

As they continued to lead their organization with emotional intelligence, Wallace and Natasha remained committed to the ongoing journey of self-awareness and self-regulation. They knew that by mastering these foundational skills, they were laying the groundwork for their continued growth and development as leaders.

As Wallace and Natasha delved deeper into the realm of emotional intelligence, they uncovered the transformative power of empathy and compassionate leadership. They understood that empathy, the ability to understand and share the feelings of others, was a cornerstone of effective leadership, fostering trust, collaboration, and a sense of belonging within their organization.

Guided by their father's teachings, they embraced empathy as a guiding principle in their leadership approach, striving to see the world through the eyes of their team members and to understand their perspectives, challenges, and aspirations. They made a conscious effort to listen actively, validate emotions, and offer support and encouragement to those in need.

In addition to empathy, Wallace and Natasha recognized the importance of compassionate leadership, which involved showing care, concern, and kindness towards others, even in the face of difficult decisions or challenging situations. They understood that compassionate leaders inspired loyalty and commitment in their team members, creating a culture of trust and psychological safety.

Wallace and Natasha practiced compassionate leadership by demonstrating empathy, understanding, and kindness in their interactions with their team members. They took the time to acknowledge the individual strengths and contributions of each team member, offering praise and recognition for their efforts and achievements.

Through their commitment to empathy and compassionate leadership, Wallace and Natasha were able to create a supportive and inclusive work environment where team members felt valued, respected, and empowered to bring their whole selves to work. They fostered a culture of belonging and collaboration, where everyone felt seen, heard, and appreciated.

As they continued to lead their organization with emotional intelligence, Wallace and Natasha remained steadfast in their commitment to empathy and compassionate leadership. They knew that by putting themselves in the shoes of their team members and leading with kindness and understanding, they were not only driving performance and productivity but also creating a workplace where people felt cared for, supported, and inspired to do their best.

As Wallace and Natasha explored further into the realm of emotional intelligence, they uncovered the crucial aspect of building resilience in times of stress. They recognized that resilience, the ability to bounce back from adversity, was essential for effective leadership, especially in challenging and uncertain times.

Drawing upon their father's wisdom, they embraced resilience as a key component of their leadership journey. They understood that leaders faced numerous obstacles and setbacks, and their ability to weather these storms with grace and determination would ultimately define their success.

Wallace and Natasha embarked on a journey to cultivate resilience within themselves and their team members. They encouraged a growth mindset, emphasizing the importance of learning from failures and setbacks rather than allowing them to derail progress.

In addition to fostering a growth mindset, Wallace and Natasha also prioritized self-care and well-being. They understood that resilience was not just about bouncing back from adversity but also about taking care of oneself in order to stay strong and focused in the face of challenges.

Wallace and Natasha practiced resilience by remaining calm and composed in stressful situations, maintaining a positive outlook, and seeking support from their team members and mentors when needed. They led by example, showing their team members that it was possible to overcome obstacles with resilience and determination.

Through their efforts to build resilience, Wallace and Natasha created a culture of strength and perseverance within their organization. Team members felt empowered to face challenges head-on, knowing that they had the support and guidance of resilient leaders to guide them through.

As they continued to lead their organization with emotional intelligence, Wallace and Natasha remained committed to fostering resilience in themselves and their team members. They knew that by building a resilient organization, they were not only better prepared to handle whatever challenges came their way but also poised for long-term success and growth.

As Wallace and Natasha delved deeper into emotional intelligence, they uncovered the profound impact of inspiring trust and loyalty as essential elements of effective leadership. They understood that trust and loyalty were not earned overnight but were the result of consistent actions and behaviors that demonstrated integrity, transparency, and authenticity.

Inspired by their father's teachings, they recognized the importance of leading with integrity and earning the trust of their team members. They made it a priority to communicate openly and honestly, sharing both the successes and challenges of the organization and being transparent about their decisions and actions.

Wallace and Natasha understood that trust was built through actions, not just words. They made promises carefully and followed through on their commitments, demonstrating reliability and accountability in their leadership. They also encouraged open communication and feedback, creating a culture of trust where team members felt comfortable sharing their thoughts and concerns.

In addition to inspiring trust, Wallace and Natasha also focused on fostering loyalty within their organization. They understood that loyalty was earned by valuing and investing in their team members, recognizing their contributions, and providing opportunities for growth and development.

Wallace and Natasha led by example, showing their team members that they were committed to their success and well-being. They offered mentorship and support, empowering their team members to take on new challenges and grow professionally. They also recognized and rewarded their team members' efforts and achievements, showing appreciation for their hard work and dedication.

Through their efforts to inspire trust and loyalty, Wallace and Natasha created a strong and cohesive team that was committed to the organization's success. Team members felt valued and appreciated, knowing that their leaders had their best interests at heart and were invested in their growth and development.

As they continued to lead their organization with emotional intelligence, Wallace and Natasha remained committed to inspiring trust and loyalty among their team members. They knew that by building a culture of trust and loyalty, they were not only fostering a positive and productive work environment but also positioning their organization for long-term success and sustainability.

As Wallace and Natasha further explored emotional intelligence, they uncovered the importance of cultivating it across the entire organization. They recognized that emotional intelligence was not just a trait for leaders but a valuable skillset for all team members, contributing to a more cohesive and empathetic workplace culture.

Inspired by their father's teachings, they embarked on a mission to foster emotional intelligence at every level of the organization. They understood that this required a multifaceted approach, including training programs, workshops, and ongoing support to help team members develop their emotional intelligence skills.

Wallace and Natasha led by example, demonstrating the principles of emotional intelligence in their interactions with team members. They encouraged open communication, active listening, and empathy, creating a culture where emotions were acknowledged and valued.

In addition to leading by example, Wallace and Natasha implemented formal training programs to help team members develop their emotional intelligence skills. They brought in experts to facilitate workshops on topics such as self-awareness, empathy, and conflict resolution, providing team members with practical tools and techniques to enhance their emotional intelligence.

Wallace and Natasha also encouraged peer-to-peer support and mentorship, creating opportunities for team members to learn from each other and share their experiences. They fostered a collaborative environment where team members felt comfortable discussing their emotions and seeking advice and support from their colleagues.

Through their efforts to cultivate emotional intelligence across the organization, Wallace and Natasha created a more resilient and empathetic workplace culture. Team members felt valued and supported, knowing that their leaders were invested in their personal and professional development.

As they continued to lead their organization with emotional intelligence, Wallace and Natasha remained committed to fostering a culture of emotional intelligence. They knew that by equipping their team members with the skills to understand and manage their emotions effectively, they were not only improving individual performance but also building a stronger and more cohesive organization overall.

# 9

# Chapter Nine: Ethical Leadership

In chapter nine, Wallace and Natasha encountered the profound importance of ethical leadership as they navigated the complexities of running their family business. They understood that ethical leadership wasn't just about making the right decisions; it was about doing what was morally right, even when faced with difficult choices and conflicting interests.

Inspired by their father's ethical principles, Wallace and Natasha embraced the responsibility of leading with integrity. They recognized that their actions as leaders had a far-reaching impact on their team members, customers, and the broader community, and they were committed to upholding the highest standards of ethical conduct.

As they faced various challenges and dilemmas in their leadership roles, Wallace and Natasha remained steadfast in their commitment to ethical leadership. They approached each decision with careful consideration, weighing the potential consequences and ensuring that their actions were aligned with their values and principles.

## CHAPTER NINE: ETHICAL LEADERSHIP

Wallace and Natasha understood that ethical leadership required courage and conviction. They were willing to stand up for what they believed was right, even in the face of opposition or adversity. They refused to compromise their integrity for short-term gain, choosing instead to prioritize long-term sustainability and trustworthiness.

In addition to leading with integrity, Wallace and Natasha also emphasized the importance of accountability and transparency in their leadership approach. They were open and honest with their team members, stakeholders, and the public, acknowledging mistakes and taking responsibility for their actions.

Through their unwavering commitment to ethical leadership, Wallace and Natasha earned the trust and respect of their team members and the broader community. They demonstrated that ethical leadership was not just a moral obligation but also a strategic advantage, leading to greater credibility, loyalty, and sustainability for their organization.

As they continued to lead their organization with integrity, Wallace and Natasha remained vigilant in their commitment to ethical leadership. They knew that by setting a positive example and upholding the highest standards of ethical conduct, they were not only safeguarding the reputation and success of their business but also making a positive impact on the world around them.

In their exploration of ethical leadership, Wallace and Natasha delved deeper into the importance of upholding integrity and honesty in every aspect of their leadership roles. They recognized that integrity was the foundation upon which trust and credibility were built, and honesty was the cornerstone of ethical conduct.

Inspired by their father's unwavering commitment to integrity, Wallace and Natasha embraced the responsibility of leading with honesty and transparency. They understood that honesty meant being truthful and forthcoming in their communications, even when the message was difficult or uncomfortable.

As they encountered various challenges and dilemmas in their leadership roles, Wallace and Natasha remained steadfast in their commitment to upholding integrity and honesty. They approached each situation with integrity, ensuring that their actions were guided by moral principles and a sense of duty to do what was right.

Wallace and Natasha knew that upholding integrity and honesty required courage and conviction. They were willing to speak up against wrongdoing and to hold themselves and others accountable for their actions. They refused to compromise their values for personal gain, choosing instead to prioritize honesty and integrity above all else.

In addition to leading with integrity and honesty, Wallace and Natasha also emphasized the importance of transparency in their leadership approach. They were open and candid with their team members, stakeholders, and the public, providing clear and accurate information and avoiding deception or manipulation.

Through their unwavering commitment to upholding integrity and honesty, Wallace and Natasha earned the trust and respect of their team members and the broader community. They demonstrated that ethical leadership was not just a moral obligation but also a strategic advantage, leading to greater credibility, loyalty, and sustainability for their organization.

As they continued to lead their organization with integrity

and honesty, Wallace and Natasha remained vigilant in their commitment to ethical leadership. They knew that by setting a positive example and upholding the highest standards of ethical conduct, they were not only safeguarding the reputation and success of their business but also making a positive impact on the world around them.

As Wallace and Natasha delved further into ethical leadership, they explored the intricacies of making ethical decisions in complex situations. They understood that ethical dilemmas often arise in the business world, requiring leaders to navigate through conflicting interests while upholding their principles.

Guided by their father's example, Wallace and Natasha embraced the challenge of making ethical decisions with integrity and clarity. They recognized that ethical decision-making involved careful consideration of the consequences and potential impact on all stakeholders involved.

As they encountered various challenges in their leadership roles, Wallace and Natasha remained resolute in their commitment to making ethical decisions. They approached each situation with a sense of responsibility, ensuring that their actions were in line with their values and principles, even when faced with difficult choices.

Wallace and Natasha understood that making ethical decisions in complex situations required moral courage and conviction. They were willing to stand by their principles and do what was right, even if it meant facing criticism or adversity.

In addition to upholding integrity in their decision-making process, Wallace and Natasha also emphasized the importance of seeking counsel and considering alternative perspectives. They understood that ethical dilemmas were rarely black and white and that consulting with trusted advisors and considering different viewpoints could help them make more informed and ethical decisions.

Through their commitment to making ethical decisions in complex situations, Wallace and Natasha earned the trust and respect of their team members and stakeholders. They demonstrated that ethical leadership was not just about following rules but about embodying principles of integrity and accountability in every aspect of their leadership roles.

As they continued to lead their organization with integrity and clarity, Wallace and Natasha remained vigilant in their commitment to ethical leadership. They knew that by making ethical decisions in complex situations, they were not only protecting the reputation and success of their business but also setting a positive example for others to follow.

As Wallace and Natasha delved deeper into the intricacies of ethical leadership, they grappled with the challenge of balancing stakeholder interests. They understood that as leaders, they were responsible for considering the needs and concerns of various stakeholders, including employees, customers, shareholders, and the broader community.

With their father's teachings as a foundation, Wallace and Natasha embraced the complexity of balancing stakeholder interests with integrity and fairness. They recognized that each stakeholder had unique perspectives and priorities, and it was their duty as leaders to consider and address these diverse interests in their decision-making process.

As they navigated through various business challenges, Wallace and Natasha remained committed to finding solutions that balanced the needs of all stakeholders involved. They sought to foster open dialogue and collaboration, inviting input and feedback from all parties to ensure that decisions were made with full consideration of their impact.

Wallace and Natasha understood that balancing stakeholder interests often required trade-offs and compromises. They were willing to make difficult decisions, weighing the potential benefits and risks to each stakeholder group and striving to find solutions that maximized overall value while minimizing harm.

In addition to considering the needs of stakeholders, Wallace and Natasha also prioritized transparency and accountability in their leadership approach. They communicated openly with all parties involved, explaining the rationale behind their decisions and addressing any concerns or objections in a respectful and constructive manner.

Through their commitment to balancing stakeholder interests, Wallace and Natasha earned the trust and respect of their team members and stakeholders. They demonstrated that ethical leadership was not just about making decisions based on personal interests or preferences but about considering the broader impact on all stakeholders involved.

As they continued to lead their organization with integrity and fairness, Wallace and Natasha remained steadfast in their commitment to balancing stakeholder interests. They knew that by prioritizing transparency, accountability, and collaboration, they were not only building a stronger and more resilient organization but also making a positive impact on the communities they served.

As Wallace and Natasha delved deeper into the realm of ethical leadership, they recognized the critical importance of promoting diversity, equity, and inclusion (DEI) within their organization. They understood that fostering a diverse and inclusive workplace was not only the right thing to do morally but also essential for driving innovation, creativity, and long-term success.

With their father's principles as their compass, Wallace and Natasha embraced the challenge of promoting DEI within their organization. They understood that diversity encompassed more than just race and gender but also encompassed differences in perspectives, backgrounds, experiences, and abilities.

As they navigated through various business challenges, Wallace and Natasha remained committed to creating a workplace where everyone felt valued, respected, and empowered to bring their authentic selves to work. They implemented policies and practices to promote diversity and inclusion at all levels of the organization, from recruitment and hiring to leadership development and decision-making processes.

Wallace and Natasha understood that promoting DEI required more than just lip service; it required tangible actions and investments. They actively sought out diverse perspectives and voices, inviting input and feedback from employees of all backgrounds and experiences. They also implemented training programs and initiatives to raise awareness and foster a culture of inclusion.

In addition to promoting diversity and inclusion internally, Wallace and Natasha also recognized the importance of championing DEI in their external relationships and partnerships. They sought out vendors, suppliers, and collaborators who shared their commitment to diversity and inclusion, aligning their business practices with their values.

Through their commitment to promoting diversity, equity, and inclusion, Wallace and Natasha created a workplace where everyone felt valued, respected, and empowered to succeed. They demonstrated that ethical leadership was not just about making decisions based on personal interests or preferences but about creating a more equitable and just society for all.

As they continued to lead their organization with integrity and compassion, Wallace and Natasha remained steadfast in their commitment to promoting diversity, equity, and inclusion. They knew that by embracing diversity and inclusion as core values of their organization, they were not only strengthening their business but also making a positive impact on the world around them.

As Wallace and Natasha delved deeper into the intricacies of ethical leadership, they recognized the importance of holding themselves and others accountable for their actions and decisions. They understood that accountability was not just about taking responsibility for one's own actions but also about ensuring that others did the same.

Guided by their father's principles, Wallace and Natasha embraced the challenge of promoting accountability within their organization. They understood that accountability fostered trust, transparency, and integrity, laying the foundation for a culture of ethical leadership.

As they encountered various challenges in their leadership roles, Wallace and Natasha remained steadfast in their commitment to holding themselves accountable. They set clear expectations and goals for their own performance, regularly evaluating their progress and taking ownership of their mistakes and shortcomings.

In addition to holding themselves accountable, Wallace and Natasha also emphasized the importance of holding others accountable for their actions. They implemented systems and processes to ensure that everyone in the organization was held to the same standards of conduct and performance.

Wallace and Natasha understood that holding others accountable required courage and consistency. They were willing to have difficult conversations and to address performance issues promptly and effectively, ensuring that everyone in the organization understood the importance of accountability.

Through their commitment to holding themselves and others accountable, Wallace and Natasha created a culture of trust and integrity within their organization. Team members felt empowered to take ownership of their work and actions, knowing that they would be held accountable for their performance.

As they continued to lead their organization with integrity and accountability, Wallace and Natasha remained vigilant in their commitment to ethical leadership. They knew that by promoting accountability at all levels of the organization, they were not only strengthening their business but also building a culture of trust, transparency, and integrity that would endure for years to come.

As Wallace and Natasha continued to explore the intricacies of ethical leadership, they recognized the pivotal role of creating a culture of ethical behavior within their organization. They understood that ethical behavior wasn't just about individual actions but also about fostering an environment where integrity, honesty, and accountability were valued and upheld by all.

Inspired by their father's teachings, Wallace and Natasha embraced the challenge of cultivating a culture of ethical behavior. They knew that building such a culture required more than just setting policies and guidelines; it required fostering an environment where ethical conduct was woven into the fabric of everyday operations.

As they navigated through various business challenges, Wallace and Natasha remained steadfast in their commitment to creating a culture of ethical behavior. They led by example, demonstrating integrity, honesty, and accountability in their own actions and decisions.

In addition to leading by example, Wallace and Natasha also implemented initiatives to promote ethical behavior across the organization. They provided training and development opportunities to help team members understand the importance of ethics in the workplace and to equip them with the knowledge and skills to make ethical decisions.

Wallace and Natasha encouraged open communication and dialogue, creating channels for team members to raise concerns and report ethical violations without fear of retaliation. They also implemented systems and processes to ensure that ethical behavior was recognized and rewarded, reinforcing the importance of integrity and honesty in the organization.

Through their commitment to creating a culture of ethical behavior, Wallace and Natasha fostered an environment where integrity, honesty, and accountability thrived. Team members felt empowered to do the right thing, knowing that ethical conduct was not only expected but also valued and rewarded.

As they continued to lead their organization with integrity and accountability, Wallace and Natasha remained dedicated to cultivating a culture of ethical behavior. They knew that by fostering an environment where ethics were prioritized and upheld, they were not only safeguarding the reputation and success of their business but also building a stronger and more resilient organization for the future.

# 10

# Chapter Ten: The Management and Prioritization

In chapter ten, Wallace and Natasha embarked on a journey to master the art of management and prioritization in their roles as leaders of their family business. As they faced increasing demands and responsibilities, they realized the critical importance of effectively managing their time, resources, and priorities to drive the success of their organization.

With their father's wisdom as their guide, Wallace and Natasha embraced the challenge of mastering management and prioritization. They understood that effective management was not just about getting things done but about strategically allocating resources and aligning actions with the organization's goals and objectives.

As they navigated through various business challenges, Wallace and Natasha remained steadfast in their commitment to mastering management and prioritization. They implemented systems and processes to streamline workflows, optimize efficiency, and maximize productivity across the organization.

In addition to managing their own time and resources, Wallace and Natasha also focused on empowering their team members to do the same. They provided training and development opportunities to help team members enhance their time management and organizational skills, ensuring that everyone was equipped to contribute effectively to the organization's success.

Wallace and Natasha understood that effective prioritization was key to achieving their goals and objectives. They identified the most important tasks and projects and allocated resources accordingly, making strategic decisions to ensure that the organization's resources were utilized effectively and efficiently.

Through their commitment to mastering management and prioritization, Wallace and Natasha transformed their organization into a well-oiled machine. They led by example, demonstrating discipline, focus, and resilience in their own work, and inspiring their team members to do the same.

As they continued to lead their organization with skill and determination, Wallace and Natasha remained dedicated to mastering management and prioritization. They knew that by effectively managing their time, resources, and priorities, they were not only driving the success of their business but also laying the foundation for a bright and prosperous future.

In their quest to master management and prioritization, Wallace and Natasha turned their attention to identifying and eliminating time wasters within their organization. They understood that time was a precious resource, and eliminating inefficiencies would allow them to focus on what truly mattered for the success of their business.

With determination in their hearts, Wallace and Natasha embarked on a thorough assessment of their organization's processes and workflows. They scrutinized every aspect of their operations, from administrative tasks to project management, seeking out inefficiencies and areas for improvement.

As they delved deeper into their analysis, Wallace and Natasha uncovered several common time wasters plaguing their organization. They identified unnecessary meetings, redundant paperwork, and inefficient communication channels as significant culprits that were sapping valuable time and resources.

Armed with this knowledge, Wallace and Natasha took decisive action to eliminate these time wasters once and for all. They streamlined their meeting schedules, implementing strict agendas and time limits to ensure that meetings were focused and productive. They also digitized and automated administrative tasks, reducing paperwork and streamlining processes for greater efficiency.

In addition to addressing internal time wasters, Wallace and Natasha also encouraged their team members to identify and eliminate inefficiencies in their own work. They provided training and support to help team members optimize their workflows and prioritize their tasks effectively, empowering them to make the most of their time.

Through their concerted efforts to identify and eliminate time wasters, Wallace and Natasha transformed their organization into a lean and agile machine. Team members felt empowered to focus on their most important tasks, knowing that unnecessary distractions had been eliminated and their time was being used effectively.

As they continued to lead their organization with determination and resolve, Wallace and Natasha remained committed to ongoing improvement and efficiency. They knew that by identifying and eliminating time wasters, they were not only maximizing productivity and performance but also creating a culture of excellence and innovation that would drive their business forward.

In their pursuit of mastering management and prioritization, Wallace and Natasha recognized the critical importance of prioritizing tasks and projects effectively. They understood that not all tasks were created equal, and focusing on the right priorities was essential for driving the success of their organization.

With determination in their hearts, Wallace and Natasha set out to develop a strategic approach to prioritization. They knew that prioritizing tasks and projects required clarity of vision, a deep understanding of their goals and objectives, and the ability to make tough decisions about where to allocate their time and resources.

As they delved into the process of prioritization, Wallace and Natasha identified their organization's key objectives and strategic initiatives. They carefully assessed each task and project against these objectives, considering factors such as urgency, importance, and potential impact on the organization's goals.

Armed with this knowledge, Wallace and Natasha developed a prioritization framework to guide their decision-making process. They categorized tasks and projects into high, medium, and low priority tiers, focusing their efforts on those activities that would deliver the greatest value and impact for their organization.

In addition to prioritizing tasks and projects at the organizational level, Wallace and Natasha also empowered their team members to prioritize their own work effectively. They provided clear guidance and expectations, helping team members understand how their individual tasks and projects aligned with the organization's broader goals and objectives.

Through their concerted efforts to prioritize tasks and projects effectively, Wallace and Natasha transformed their organization into a well-oiled machine. Team members felt empowered to focus their efforts on the most important priorities, knowing that their work was aligned with the organization's strategic vision and goals.

As they continued to lead their organization with determination and foresight, Wallace and Natasha remained committed to the ongoing process of prioritization. They knew that by focusing their time and resources on the right priorities, they were not only driving the success of their business but also laying the foundation for sustainable growth and prosperity in the years to come.

In their journey to master management and prioritization, Wallace and Natasha understood the importance of setting boundaries and managing interruptions effectively. They recognized that maintaining focus and productivity required creating an environment that minimized distractions and interruptions.

With determination in their hearts, Wallace and Natasha set out to establish clear boundaries for themselves and their team members. They defined designated work hours and communication protocols, ensuring that everyone understood when it was appropriate to interrupt and when it was not.

As they delved into the process of setting boundaries, Wallace and Natasha identified common sources of interruptions within their organization. They recognized that constant email notifications, impromptu meetings, and unstructured communication channels were significant culprits that disrupted their workflow and productivity.

Armed with this knowledge, Wallace and Natasha implemented strategies to manage interruptions effectively. They encouraged team members to block off focused work time in their calendars, minimizing interruptions and allowing for deep concentration on important tasks and projects.

In addition to setting boundaries for themselves and their team members, Wallace and Natasha also led by example, demonstrating discipline and respect for boundaries in their own work habits. They designated specific times for checking emails and attending meetings, ensuring that they remained focused on their most important priorities.

Through their concerted efforts to set boundaries and manage interruptions, Wallace and Natasha created a more productive and focused work environment within their organization. Team members felt empowered to prioritize their work and minimize distractions, knowing that their leaders supported their efforts to maintain focus and productivity.

As they continued to lead their organization with determination and foresight, Wallace and Natasha remained committed to the ongoing process of setting boundaries and managing interruptions. They knew that by creating an environment that prioritized focus and productivity, they were not only driving the success of their business but also fostering a culture of excellence and innovation that would endure for years to come.

In their pursuit of mastering management and prioritization, Wallace and Natasha understood the power of leveraging time management tools and techniques to enhance their productivity and efficiency. They recognized that in today's fast-paced world, having the right tools at their disposal could make all the difference in how effectively they managed their time.

With determination in their hearts, Wallace and Natasha set out to explore a variety of time management tools and techniques. They sought out software applications, such as task management platforms and calendar apps, that could help them organize their tasks, schedule their time, and track their progress.

As they delved into the world of time management tools, Wallace and Natasha discovered a wealth of options available to them. They experimented with different tools and techniques, seeking out those that best suited their needs and preferences.

Armed with this newfound knowledge, Wallace and Natasha implemented time management tools and techniques into their daily routines. They used task management platforms to create to-do lists and prioritize their tasks effectively. They utilized calendar apps to schedule their time strategically, blocking off dedicated time for focused work and important meetings.

In addition to leveraging technology, Wallace and Natasha also embraced timeless time management techniques, such as the Pomodoro Technique and the Eisenhower Matrix. They used these techniques to break their work into manageable chunks, prioritize their tasks, and maximize their productivity throughout the day.

Through their concerted efforts to use time management tools and techniques, Wallace and Natasha experienced a significant improvement in their productivity and efficiency. They felt more organized and in control of their time, allowing them to focus their efforts on the most important priorities for their organization.

As they continued to lead their organization with determination and foresight, Wallace and Natasha remained committed to the ongoing process of refining their time management skills. They knew that by leveraging the right tools and techniques, they were not only driving the success of their business but also setting themselves up for continued growth and prosperity in the future.

In their quest to master management and prioritization, Wallace and Natasha recognized the importance of practicing work-life balance. They understood that maintaining a healthy balance between work and personal life was essential for their well-being and long-term success.

With determination in their hearts, Wallace and Natasha set out to prioritize their own well-being and encourage a culture of balance within their organization. They recognized that being overworked and burnt out would ultimately hinder their ability to lead effectively and drive the success of their business.

As they delved into the practice of work-life balance, Wallace and Natasha identified areas where they could make improvements in their own lives. They committed to setting boundaries around their work hours, carving out dedicated time for rest, relaxation, and time spent with family and friends.

Armed with this newfound commitment to balance, Wallace and Natasha led by example, demonstrating to their team members the importance of prioritizing well-being alongside professional success. They encouraged team members to take breaks, disconnect from work during off-hours, and prioritize self-care activities.

In addition to promoting work-life balance for themselves and their team members, Wallace and Natasha also implemented policies and initiatives to support a healthy work-life balance within their organization. They offered flexible work arrangements, such as remote work options and flexible hours, to accommodate the diverse needs of their team members.

Through their concerted efforts to practice work-life balance, Wallace and Natasha experienced greater fulfillment and satisfaction in both their personal and professional lives. They found that by prioritizing their well-being, they were able to lead with clarity, focus, and resilience, driving the success of their business forward.

As they continued to lead their organization with determination and foresight, Wallace and Natasha remained committed to promoting a culture of work-life balance. They knew that by prioritizing the well-being of their team members, they were not only fostering a happier and healthier workplace but also laying the foundation for long-term success and sustainability.

In their journey to master management and prioritization, Wallace and Natasha recognized the importance of fostering a culture of time consciousness within their organization. They understood that respecting time, both their own and that of their team members, was essential for maximizing productivity and efficiency.

With determination in their hearts, Wallace and Natasha set out to instill a sense of time consciousness throughout their organization. They knew that being mindful of time would help everyone make the most of their resources and achieve their goals more effectively.

As they delved into the practice of fostering a culture of time consciousness, Wallace and Natasha implemented various strategies to encourage their team members to respect and value time. They led by example, arriving promptly to meetings and appointments and adhering to deadlines with diligence.

Armed with this commitment to time consciousness, Wallace and Natasha communicated the importance of punctuality and efficiency to their team members. They emphasized the impact that being mindful of time could have on the success of their organization and encouraged everyone to prioritize their tasks and manage their time effectively.

In addition to promoting time consciousness within their organization, Wallace and Natasha implemented tools and processes to help their team members track and manage their time more effectively. They provided training and resources on time management techniques and encouraged regular reflection on how time was being spent.

Through their concerted efforts to foster a culture of time consciousness, Wallace and Natasha saw a positive shift in their organization. Team members became more mindful of how they utilized their time, making conscious efforts to minimize distractions and focus on their most important tasks.

As they continued to lead their organization with determination and foresight, Wallace and Natasha remained committed to promoting a culture of time consciousness. They knew that by instilling a sense of respect for time within their organization, they were not only driving productivity and efficiency but also creating a workplace where everyone could thrive and succeed.

# 11

# Chapter Eleven: Motivating and Inspiring

In chapter eleven, Wallace and Natasha embarked on a mission to master the art of motivating and inspiring others within their organization. They understood that motivation was the fuel that propelled their team members to achieve greatness and drive the success of their business forward.

With determination in their hearts, Wallace and Natasha set out to cultivate a culture of motivation and inspiration within their organization. They knew that by empowering their team members and igniting their passion, they could unlock their full potential and achieve extraordinary results.

As they delved into the practice of motivating and inspiring others, Wallace and Natasha embraced a variety of strategies to foster engagement and enthusiasm among their team members. They recognized that different individuals were motivated by different things, and they tailored their approach accordingly.

Armed with this understanding, Wallace and Natasha implemented initiatives to recognize and celebrate the achievements of their team members. They praised their efforts publicly, highlighting their contributions and acknowledging their impact on the organization's success.

In addition to recognition, Wallace and Natasha also provided opportunities for growth and development, empowering their team members to stretch beyond their comfort zones and pursue their aspirations. They offered mentorship and coaching, helping team members set and achieve ambitious goals for themselves.

Through their concerted efforts to motivate and inspire others, Wallace and Natasha witnessed a remarkable transformation within their organization. Team members became more engaged and passionate about their work, going above and beyond to deliver exceptional results and drive the success of the business forward.

As they continued to lead their organization with determination and foresight, Wallace and Natasha remained committed to igniting inspiration in others. They knew that by fostering a culture of motivation and empowerment, they were not only driving the success of their business but also creating a community where everyone could thrive and achieve their full potential.

In their pursuit to master the art of motivating and inspiring others, Wallace and Natasha recognized the importance of understanding motivation theory. They understood that delving into the principles of motivation would provide them with valuable insights into what drove their team members and how they could effectively ignite their passion.

With determination in their hearts, Wallace and Natasha delved into the study of motivation theory, eager to uncover the underlying factors that influenced human behavior and engagement. They explored various theories, from Maslow's hierarchy of needs to Herzberg's two-factor theory, seeking to understand the complex interplay of intrinsic and extrinsic motivators.

As they delved deeper into motivation theory, Wallace and Natasha gained a deeper understanding of what drove their team members and how they could leverage this knowledge to inspire greatness. They recognized that different individuals were motivated by different factors, and they tailored their approach accordingly.

Armed with this newfound understanding, Wallace and Natasha implemented strategies to tap into the intrinsic motivations of their team members. They created a sense of purpose and meaning within their organization, aligning individual goals with the broader mission and vision of the company.

In addition to intrinsic motivators, Wallace and Natasha also leveraged extrinsic motivators to inspire their team members. They offered incentives and rewards for exceptional performance, recognizing and celebrating the achievements of their team members in meaningful ways.

Through their concerted efforts to understand motivation theory, Wallace and Natasha saw a profound impact on their organization. Team members became more engaged and committed to their work, driven by a sense of purpose and fulfillment that transcended traditional rewards and incentives.

As they continued to lead their organization with determination and foresight, Wallace and Natasha remained committed to applying their understanding of motivation theory to inspire greatness in others. They knew that by tapping into the intrinsic motivations of their team members, they could create a culture of passion and excellence that would propel their business to new heights.

In their quest to inspire greatness within their organization, Wallace and Natasha understood the importance of tailoring motivational strategies to individuals. They recognized that each team member had unique needs, preferences, and aspirations, and they were determined to customize their approach accordingly.

With determination in their hearts, Wallace and Natasha set out to build strong relationships with each member of their team, taking the time to understand their individual motivations and drivers. They engaged in open and honest conversations, listening attentively to their team members' aspirations and concerns.

As they delved into the process of tailoring motivational strategies, Wallace and Natasha discovered that different individuals were motivated by different things. Some were driven by a desire for recognition and advancement, while others were motivated by a sense of purpose and meaning in their work.

Armed with this insight, Wallace and Natasha developed personalized motivational plans for each member of their team. They identified specific goals and aspirations for each individual and worked collaboratively to create strategies to help them achieve their full potential.

In addition to individual goal setting, Wallace and Natasha also provided ongoing support and encouragement to their team members. They offered mentorship and coaching, helping each individual overcome obstacles and develop the skills and confidence needed to succeed.

Through their concerted efforts to tailor motivational strategies to individuals, Wallace and Natasha witnessed a remarkable transformation within their organization. Team members felt valued and empowered, motivated to go above and beyond to achieve their goals and drive the success of the business forward.

As they continued to lead their organization with determination and foresight, Wallace and Natasha remained committed to the ongoing process of personalizing motivational strategies. They knew that by understanding and addressing the unique motivations of each team member, they could create a culture of engagement and excellence that would propel their business to new heights.

In their relentless pursuit of inspiring greatness within their organization, Wallace and Natasha recognized the profound impact of providing meaningful recognition and rewards to their team members. They understood that acknowledging and celebrating achievements was essential for fostering a culture of engagement and motivation.

With determination burning bright in their hearts, Wallace and Natasha set out to implement a system of recognition and rewards that would truly resonate with their team members. They knew that generic gestures would not suffice; instead, they sought to provide personalized recognition that would make each individual feel valued and appreciated.

As they delved into the process of providing meaningful recognition and rewards, Wallace and Natasha took the time to understand what truly mattered to each member of their team. They engaged in open dialogue, listening attentively to their team members' preferences and aspirations.

Armed with this insight, Wallace and Natasha developed a variety of recognition and reward initiatives tailored to the unique preferences and motivations of their team members.

For some, public acknowledgment of their achievements in team meetings or company-wide communications was highly meaningful. For others, a private one-on-one conversation or handwritten note of appreciation held greater significance.

In addition to personalized recognition, Wallace and Natasha also offered tangible rewards that aligned with the interests and preferences of their team members. They provided opportunities for professional development, flexible work arrangements, and even non-monetary perks such as extra vacation days or tickets to events.

Through their concerted efforts to provide meaningful recognition and rewards, Wallace and Natasha witnessed a profound transformation within their organization. Team members felt valued and respected, their morale lifted by the genuine appreciation shown for their hard work and dedication.

As they continued to lead their organization with determination and foresight, Wallace and Natasha remained committed to the ongoing process of providing meaningful recognition and rewards. They knew that by acknowledging and celebrating achievements in a meaningful way, they could inspire their team members to reach new heights of excellence and drive the success of the business forward.

In their unwavering dedication to inspiring greatness within their organization, Wallace and Natasha recognized the importance of creating a sense of purpose and ownership among their team members. They understood that when individuals felt connected to a greater mission and empowered to take ownership of their work, they were more motivated, engaged, and committed to achieving success.

With determination blazing in their hearts, Wallace and

Natasha set out to instill a deep sense of purpose and ownership within their team. They knew that it was essential for every team member to understand how their contributions fit into the broader vision of the organization and to feel a sense of personal investment in its success.

As they delved into the process of creating a sense of purpose and ownership, Wallace and Natasha engaged their team members in meaningful conversations about the company's mission, values, and goals. They highlighted the impact that each individual's work had on achieving these objectives, emphasizing the importance of their contributions.

Armed with this understanding, Wallace and Natasha empowered their team members to take ownership of their work and make meaningful contributions to the organization's success. They encouraged autonomy and decision-making, trusting their team members to take initiative and drive projects forward.

In addition to fostering a sense of ownership, Wallace and Natasha also worked to create a culture where every team member felt a deep sense of purpose in their work. They aligned individual goals with the company's mission and values, helping team members see how their work directly contributed to making a positive impact in the world.

Through their concerted efforts to create a sense of purpose and ownership, Wallace and Natasha witnessed a profound transformation within their organization. Team members felt empowered and motivated, united by a shared sense of purpose and a collective commitment to achieving the organization's goals.

As they continued to lead their organization with determination and foresight, Wallace and Natasha remained committed to fostering a culture of purpose and ownership. They knew that by empowering their team members to take ownership of their work and connect it to a greater mission, they could inspire greatness and drive the success of the business forward.

In their relentless pursuit of inspiring greatness within their organization, Wallace and Natasha understood the immense power of leading by example and inspiring excellence in others. They recognized that their actions spoke louder than words and that by modeling the behaviors and values they wished to see in their team members, they could ignite a spark of inspiration that would drive the entire organization forward.

With determination blazing in their hearts, Wallace and Natasha set out to exemplify the qualities of leadership and excellence they hoped to instill in their team. They embraced a mindset of continuous growth and improvement, constantly challenging themselves to raise the bar and set new standards of excellence.

As they delved into the process of leading by example and inspiring excellence, Wallace and Natasha took every opportunity to demonstrate their commitment to the organization's mission and values. They approached their work with passion and dedication, tackling challenges head-on and never settling for mediocrity.

Armed with this commitment to excellence, Wallace and Natasha inspired their team members to strive for greatness in everything they did. They led by example, showing their team members what was possible when they pushed beyond their limits and pursued their goals with unwavering determination.

In addition to modeling excellence in their own work, Wallace and Natasha also provided mentorship and guidance to their team members, helping them unlock their full potential and achieve their aspirations. They offered support and encouragement, empowering their team members to take risks and embrace new opportunities for growth.

Through their concerted efforts to lead by example and inspire excellence, Wallace and Natasha witnessed a remarkable transformation within their organization. Team members were inspired to reach new heights of performance and achievement, driven by the example set by their leaders.

As they continued to lead their organization with determination and foresight, Wallace and Natasha remained committed to upholding the highest standards of excellence and inspiring greatness in others. They knew that by leading by example and fostering a culture of excellence, they could create a workplace where everyone could thrive and achieve their full potential.

In their quest to inspire greatness within their organization, Wallace and Natasha understood the importance of sustaining motivation through continuous engagement. They recognized that motivation was not a one-time effort but rather an ongoing process that required consistent attention and nurturing.

With determination burning bright in their hearts, Wallace and Natasha set out to create a culture of continuous engagement within their team. They knew that by keeping their team members engaged and invested in their work, they could maintain high levels of motivation and drive sustained success.

As they delved into the process of sustaining motivation through continuous engagement, Wallace and Natasha implemented various initiatives to keep their team members connected and enthusiastic about their work. They fostered open communication channels, encouraging regular feedback and dialogue to address any concerns and keep everyone aligned with the organization's goals.

Armed with this commitment to continuous engagement, Wallace and Natasha sought to create opportunities for their team members to grow and develop professionally. They provided ongoing training and development opportunities, empowering their team members to expand their skills and advance their careers within the organization.

In addition to professional development, Wallace and Natasha also prioritized creating a supportive and inclusive work environment where every team member felt valued and respected. They celebrated diversity and encouraged collaboration, recognizing that a sense of belonging was essential for maintaining motivation and engagement.

Through their concerted efforts to sustain motivation through continuous engagement, Wallace and Natasha witnessed a profound transformation within their organization. Team members remained motivated and enthusiastic about their work, driven by a sense of purpose and connection to the organization's mission.

As they continued to lead their organization with determination and foresight, Wallace and Natasha remained committed to the ongoing process of sustaining motivation through continuous engagement. They knew that by keeping their team members engaged and invested in their work, they could create a culture of excellence and drive sustained success for years to come.

# 12

# Chapter Twelve: Resolving Conflict and Negotiation

In Chapter Twelve, Wallace and Natasha confronted the inevitable reality of conflict within their organization. Despite their best efforts to foster a positive and collaborative environment, tensions arose, and disagreements emerged among team members. Recognizing the importance of effectively resolving conflict and negotiation, Wallace and Natasha embarked on a journey to restore harmony and promote productive relationships within their team.

With determination in their hearts, Wallace and Natasha faced the challenge head-on, understanding that conflict, when handled constructively, could lead to growth and innovation. They approached the situation with empathy and a commitment to understanding the underlying causes of the conflict.

As they delved into the process of resolving conflict and negotiation, Wallace and Natasha facilitated open and honest discussions among the parties involved. They encouraged active listening and sought to uncover the root causes of the conflict, recognizing that effective resolution required addressing underlying issues.

Armed with this understanding, Wallace and Natasha employed various conflict resolution techniques, including mediation and compromise, to find mutually acceptable solutions. They encouraged collaboration and sought win-win outcomes that honored the interests of all parties involved.

In addition to resolving existing conflicts, Wallace and Natasha also implemented strategies to prevent future conflicts from arising. They promoted clear communication, established guidelines for constructive feedback, and fostered a culture of respect and understanding within their team.

Through their concerted efforts to resolve conflict and negotiation, Wallace and Natasha witnessed a remarkable transformation within their organization. Team members learned to address differences constructively, turning conflict into opportunities for growth and innovation.

As they continued to lead their organization with determination and foresight, Wallace and Natasha remained committed to promoting harmony and productive relationships within their team. They knew that by effectively resolving conflict and negotiation, they could create a culture of trust and collaboration that would propel their business to new heights of success.

In their pursuit of harmony and cohesion within the organization, Wallace and Natasha delved into the intricate process of identifying the sources of conflict. They understood that to effectively resolve conflicts, they first needed to unearth the underlying causes that fueled discord among team members.

With unwavering determination, Wallace and Natasha embarked on a journey to uncover the roots of conflict within their organization. They conducted thorough investigations, engaging in open conversations with team members and carefully analyzing past incidents to gain insights into the origins of discord.

As they delved deeper into the process, Wallace and Natasha discovered that conflicts often stemmed from a variety of sources, ranging from miscommunication and differing perspectives to competing priorities and personal differences. They realized that by identifying these underlying factors, they could address conflicts at their core and prevent future discord.

Armed with this understanding, Wallace and Natasha employed a variety of tools and techniques to pinpoint the sources of conflict. They conducted surveys to gather feedback from team members, facilitated group discussions to encourage open dialogue, and sought input from external experts to gain fresh perspectives.

In addition to these proactive measures, Wallace and Natasha also encouraged team members to express their concerns openly and honestly, creating a safe and supportive environment for communication. They recognized that by fostering transparency and trust, they could uncover hidden sources of conflict and pave the way for resolution.

Through their concerted efforts to identify the sources of conflict, Wallace and Natasha gained valuable insights into the dynamics of their organization. They learned to recognize patterns and trends, enabling them to address conflicts more effectively and promote a culture of harmony and collaboration.

As they continued to lead their organization with determination and foresight, Wallace and Natasha remained committed to ongoing efforts to identify and address the sources of conflict. They knew that by proactively addressing underlying issues, they could create a workplace where conflicts were resolved swiftly and constructively, fostering a culture of unity and resilience.

In their quest to foster harmony and cohesion within the organization, Wallace and Natasha embarked on the crucial task of choosing the right conflict resolution approach. They understood that each conflict was unique, requiring a tailored approach to effectively address the underlying issues and restore productive relationships among team members.

With unwavering determination, Wallace and Natasha delved into the process of evaluating different conflict resolution approaches, weighing the strengths and limitations of each option. They recognized that the key to successful conflict resolution lay in selecting the approach best suited to the specific circumstances and dynamics of the conflict at hand.

As they navigated the complexities of choosing the right approach, Wallace and Natasha considered factors such as the nature of the conflict, the personalities involved, and the desired outcomes. They understood that some conflicts might be best resolved through direct communication and negotiation, while others might require the intervention of a neutral mediator or facilitator.

Armed with this understanding, Wallace and Natasha carefully assessed their options and selected the most appropriate conflict resolution approach for each situation. They employed a variety of techniques, including mediation, negotiation, collaboration, and compromise, depending on the unique circumstances of each conflict.

In addition to choosing the right approach, Wallace and Natasha also recognized the importance of involving all parties in the resolution process. They ensured that team members had a voice in the decision-making process and were empowered to contribute their perspectives and ideas to finding a resolution.

Through their concerted efforts to choose the right conflict resolution approach, Wallace and Natasha successfully navigated the path to resolution, fostering constructive dialogue and reaching mutually acceptable outcomes. They demonstrated their commitment to promoting harmony and collaboration within their organization, laying the foundation for continued success and growth.

As they continued to lead their organization with determination and foresight, Wallace and Natasha remained vigilant in their efforts to address conflicts promptly and effectively. They knew that by choosing the right conflict resolution approach, they could create a culture where differences were respected, conflicts were resolved constructively, and relationships flourished.

In their endeavor to foster harmony and resolve conflicts within the organization, Wallace and Natasha recognized the power of facilitating collaborative problem-solving. They understood that by harnessing the collective wisdom and expertise of their team members, they could generate innovative solutions and foster a sense of ownership and unity.

With unwavering determination, Wallace and Natasha embarked on the journey of facilitating collaborative problem-solving, inviting team members to participate in a process of collective brainstorming and idea generation. They understood that by involving team members in the problem-solving process, they could tap into diverse perspectives and experiences, leading to more robust and creative solutions.

As they delved into the process, Wallace and Natasha created a supportive and inclusive environment where team members felt empowered to contribute their ideas and insights. They encouraged open communication and active listening, ensuring that every voice was heard and respected.

Armed with this commitment to collaboration, Wallace and Natasha guided their team members through a structured problem-solving process, breaking down complex issues into manageable steps and encouraging creative thinking and innovation. They facilitated brainstorming sessions, conducted group discussions, and encouraged team members to explore multiple perspectives and approaches to problem-solving.

In addition to facilitating collaboration among team members, Wallace and Natasha also fostered a culture of trust and mutual respect, where differences of opinion were embraced as opportunities for learning and growth. They encouraged constructive feedback and dialogue, recognizing that conflict could be a catalyst for positive change when approached with openness and humility.

Through their concerted efforts to facilitate collaborative problem-solving, Wallace and Natasha witnessed a remarkable transformation within their organization. Team members came together, united by a shared sense of purpose and a commitment to finding solutions to complex challenges.

As they continued to lead their organization with determination and foresight, Wallace and Natasha remained committed to harnessing the power of collaborative problem-solving. They knew that by fostering a culture of collaboration and innovation, they could overcome any obstacle and achieve their shared goals with confidence and resilience.

In their mission to foster harmony and resolve conflicts within the organization, Wallace and Natasha recognized the significance of negotiating win-win solutions. They understood that successful negotiation required a balance between assertiveness and cooperation, aiming to achieve outcomes that satisfied the needs and interests of all parties involved.

With unwavering determination, Wallace and Natasha embarked on the path of negotiating win-win solutions, seeking to create mutually beneficial agreements that would uphold the integrity of relationships and promote long-term collaboration.

As they delved into the process, Wallace and Natasha approached negotiations with empathy and a commitment to understanding the perspectives and motivations of all stakeholders. They recognized that by acknowledging and respecting the interests of others, they could build trust and goodwill, laying the foundation for successful negotiation.

Armed with this understanding, Wallace and Natasha employed a variety of negotiation techniques to craft win-win solutions. They engaged in active listening, seeking to understand the underlying needs and concerns of all parties, and used creative problem-solving to explore alternative solutions that would satisfy everyone's interests.

In addition to their collaborative approach, Wallace and Natasha also demonstrated assertiveness and confidence in advocating for their own interests and priorities. They communicated their needs clearly and persuasively, while remaining open to compromise and flexibility in pursuit of a mutually acceptable outcome.

Through their concerted efforts to negotiate win-win solutions, Wallace and Natasha achieved remarkable results, forging agreements that satisfied the needs and interests of all parties involved. They demonstrated their commitment to fostering positive relationships and promoting collaboration within their organization.

As they continued to lead their organization with determination and foresight, Wallace and Natasha remained steadfast in their commitment to negotiating win-win solutions. They knew that by prioritizing collaboration and mutual benefit, they could resolve conflicts constructively and pave the way for greater success and prosperity in the future.

In their relentless pursuit of harmony and resolution within the organization, Wallace and Natasha understood the importance of mediating disputes fairly and impartially. They recognized that effective mediation required a delicate balance of empathy, neutrality, and diplomacy to facilitate constructive dialogue and reach mutually acceptable resolutions.

With unwavering determination, Wallace and Natasha embraced the role of mediators, committed to guiding conflicting parties towards reconciliation and understanding. They approached each dispute with an open mind and a compassionate heart, seeking to foster an environment where all voices could be heard and respected.

As they delved into the process, Wallace and Natasha employed a variety of mediation techniques to facilitate productive discussions and find common ground. They encouraged open communication, active listening, and empathy, creating a safe space for conflicting parties to express their concerns and perspectives without fear of judgment.

Armed with this commitment to fairness and impartiality, Wallace and Natasha remained neutral and objective throughout the mediation process, refraining from taking sides or imposing their own opinions. They maintained a focus on the underlying interests and needs of all parties involved, guiding them towards mutually beneficial solutions.

In addition to their role as mediators, Wallace and Natasha provided support and encouragement to conflicting parties, helping them navigate through challenging emotions and find constructive ways to address their differences. They remained patient and persistent, committed to guiding them towards resolution with dignity and respect.

Through their concerted efforts to mediate disputes fairly and impartially, Wallace and Natasha witnessed remarkable transformations within the organization. Conflicting parties were able to set aside their differences and find common ground, paving the way for renewed collaboration and harmony.

As they continued to lead their organization with determination and foresight, Wallace and Natasha remained steadfast in their commitment to mediating disputes fairly and impartially. They knew that by fostering a culture of respect and understanding, they could overcome any obstacle and achieve their shared goals with unity and resilience.

In their relentless pursuit of harmony and resolution within the organization, Wallace and Natasha confronted the daunting task of restoring trust and rebuilding relationships after conflict. They understood that conflicts could leave lasting scars and erode trust between team members, but they remained determined to heal wounds and mend bridges.

With unwavering determination, Wallace and Natasha embarked on the challenging journey of restoring trust and rebuilding relationships, recognizing that it would require patience, empathy, and genuine effort from all parties involved.

As they delved into the process, Wallace and Natasha approached each relationship with care and compassion, acknowledging the hurt and disappointment that conflicts had caused. They extended olive branches of reconciliation, offering heartfelt apologies and demonstrating a genuine willingness to listen and understand.

Armed with this commitment to healing, Wallace and Natasha engaged in open and honest conversations with those affected by conflict, seeking to address underlying grievances and rebuild trust from the ground up. They acknowledged past mistakes and shortcomings, and they committed to fostering an environment of mutual respect and support.

In addition to their efforts to repair individual relationships, Wallace and Natasha also implemented initiatives to promote unity and collaboration within the organization as a whole. They organized team-building activities, facilitated group discussions, and encouraged team members to work together towards common goals.

Through their concerted efforts to restore trust and rebuild relationships, Wallace and Natasha witnessed remarkable transformations within the organization. Team members began to let go of past grievances and embrace a spirit of forgiveness and reconciliation, paving the way for renewed cooperation and camaraderie.

As they continued to lead their organization with determination and foresight, Wallace and Natasha remained steadfast in their commitment to restoring trust and rebuilding relationships after conflict. They knew that by fostering a culture of understanding and forgiveness, they could create a stronger, more resilient organization where conflicts were resolved constructively, and relationships flourished.

# 13

# Chapter Thirteen: Building Resilience and Managing Stress

In the tumultuous journey of leading their family business, Wallace and Natasha encountered numerous challenges that tested their resilience and ability to manage stress. As they navigated the highs and lows of entrepreneurship, they realized the importance of building resilience and developing effective stress management strategies to thrive in the face of adversity.

With determination in their hearts, Wallace and Natasha embarked on the transformative journey of building resilience and managing stress, recognizing that their ability to bounce back from setbacks would be crucial to their success as leaders.

As they delved into the process, Wallace and Natasha confronted their own vulnerabilities and fears, acknowledging that even the most resilient leaders experienced moments of doubt and uncertainty. They embraced the concept of resilience as a skill that could be cultivated and strengthened over time through practice and self-awareness.

Armed with this understanding, Wallace and Natasha explored various techniques and practices to build resilience and manage stress effectively. They prioritized self-care, incorporating regular exercise, healthy eating, and mindfulness into their daily routines to nurture their physical and mental well-being.

In addition to these personal practices, Wallace and Natasha also focused on fostering a culture of resilience within their organization. They encouraged open communication and transparency, creating an environment where team members felt supported and empowered to seek help when needed.

Through their concerted efforts to build resilience and manage stress, Wallace and Natasha discovered newfound strength and resilience within themselves and their team. They learned to embrace challenges as opportunities for growth and innovation, rather than obstacles to be feared.

As they continued to lead their organization with determination and foresight, Wallace and Natasha remained committed to prioritizing their well-being and the well-being of their team. They knew that by building resilience and managing stress effectively, they could weather any storm and emerge stronger, more resilient leaders in the face of adversity.

As Wallace and Natasha delved deeper into their journey of resilience and stress management, they encountered the ominous specter of burnout lurking in the shadows. They understood that in the fast-paced world of entrepreneurship, the pressures and demands of leadership could take a toll on their mental and emotional well-being, leading to burnout if left unchecked.

With a sense of urgency, Wallace and Natasha turned their attention to recognizing the signs of burnout and stress, determined to safeguard their own health and the well-being of their team members.

As they delved into the process, Wallace and Natasha became attuned to the subtle indicators of burnout, from persistent fatigue and irritability to feelings of detachment and cynicism. They acknowledged that burnout could manifest in different ways for each individual, requiring a keen eye and a compassionate heart to recognize.

Armed with this awareness, Wallace and Natasha created a culture of openness and honesty within their organization, where team members felt comfortable discussing their struggles and seeking support when needed. They encouraged regular check-ins and one-on-one conversations, providing a safe space for individuals to express their concerns and seek guidance.

In addition to their efforts to support their team members, Wallace and Natasha also prioritized self-care and self-awareness, recognizing that they too were susceptible to burnout. They committed to practicing mindfulness, setting boundaries, and seeking help when needed, knowing that they couldn't lead effectively if they neglected their own well-being.

Through their concerted efforts to recognize the signs of burnout and stress, Wallace and Natasha empowered themselves and their team members to navigate the depths of burnout with resilience and grace. They learned to prioritize self-care and seek support when needed, knowing that by taking care of themselves, they could better serve their organization and lead with clarity and compassion.

As they continued to lead their organization with determination and foresight, Wallace and Natasha remained vigilant in their efforts to recognize the signs of burnout and stress, knowing that by addressing these challenges proactively, they could create a culture where well-being was valued and supported.

In their quest for resilience and stress management, Wallace and Natasha unearthed the invaluable practice of self-care and stress management. They understood that amidst the chaos of leadership, prioritizing their well-being was not a luxury but a necessity for sustained success and fulfillment.

With a renewed sense of purpose, Wallace and Natasha embraced the art of self-care and stress management, recognizing that nurturing their own souls was paramount to leading their organization effectively.

As they delved into the process, Wallace and Natasha explored various practices to cultivate self-care and manage stress, from mindfulness meditation and yoga to journaling and spending time in nature. They recognized that self-care looked different for everyone and encouraged their team members to find activities that nourished their minds, bodies, and spirits.

Armed with this commitment to self-care, Wallace and Natasha carved out time in their busy schedules to prioritize activities that brought them joy and replenished their energy. They set boundaries around work hours, delegated tasks when necessary, and made time for rest and relaxation, knowing that they couldn't pour from an empty cup.

In addition to their personal practices, Wallace and Natasha also integrated stress management techniques into their leadership approach, fostering a culture where well-being was valued and supported. They encouraged regular breaks, promoted work-life balance, and provided resources for managing stress effectively.

Through their concerted efforts to practice self-care and stress management, Wallace and Natasha discovered newfound resilience and vitality within themselves and their organization.

They learned to navigate the ups and downs of leadership with grace and resilience, knowing that by taking care of themselves, they could better serve their team and lead with clarity and compassion.

As they continued to lead their organization with determination and foresight, Wallace and Natasha remained committed to prioritizing self-care and stress management, knowing that by nurturing their own souls, they could create a culture where well-being thrived, and success followed suit.

As Wallace and Natasha delved deeper into their journey of resilience and stress management, they recognized the profound impact of cultivating a supportive work environment. They understood that a culture of support and encouragement could serve as a powerful buffer against the challenges of leadership, fostering resilience and well-being among their team members.

With unwavering determination, Wallace and Natasha set out to create a haven of support within their organization, where team members felt valued, empowered, and cared for.

As they delved into the process, Wallace and Natasha implemented various initiatives to cultivate a supportive work environment. They encouraged open communication and transparency, creating channels for team members to share their concerns, ideas, and successes freely. They also fostered a culture of collaboration and teamwork, where individuals felt supported and encouraged to lean on one another during challenging times.

Armed with this commitment to support, Wallace and Natasha provided resources and opportunities for personal and professional growth, investing in training programs, mentorship initiatives, and employee assistance programs. They recognized that by equipping their team members with the tools and support they needed to thrive, they could cultivate a resilient and high-performing workforce.

In addition to their efforts to support their team members, Wallace and Natasha led by example, modeling vulnerability and authenticity in their own leadership approach. They shared their own struggles and challenges openly, creating a culture where vulnerability was embraced and seen as a strength.

Through their concerted efforts to cultivate a supportive work environment, Wallace and Natasha witnessed remarkable transformations within their organization. Team members felt a sense of belonging and camaraderie, knowing that they were valued and supported by their leaders and peers.

As they continued to lead their organization with determination and foresight, Wallace and Natasha remained steadfast in their commitment to fostering a culture of support and encouragement. They knew that by creating a supportive work environment, they could empower their team members to overcome any obstacle and achieve their full potential, both personally and professionally.

In their journey of resilience and stress management, Wallace and Natasha confronted the pervasive silence surrounding mental health in the workplace. They understood that mental health challenges were often shrouded in stigma and shame, preventing individuals from seeking help and support when needed.

With unwavering resolve, Wallace and Natasha embarked on a mission to break the silence and encourage open dialogue about mental health within their organization. They recognized that fostering a culture of empathy and understanding was essential to supporting the well-being of their team members.

As they delved into the process, Wallace and Natasha initiated conversations about mental health, creating spaces for team members to share their experiences, struggles, and triumphs without fear of judgment. They emphasized the importance of empathy and compassion, encouraging team members to listen actively and offer support to those in need.

Armed with this commitment to openness and understanding, Wallace and Natasha provided resources and support for mental health within their organization. They implemented training programs to raise awareness about mental health issues and equip team members with the tools and knowledge to support themselves and their colleagues.

In addition to their efforts to promote mental health awareness, Wallace and Natasha led by example, prioritizing their own well-being and openly discussing their experiences with mental health challenges. They shared stories of resilience and recovery, demonstrating that seeking help was a sign of strength, not weakness.

Through their concerted efforts to encourage open dialogue about mental health, Wallace and Natasha created a culture where individuals felt supported and empowered to prioritize their mental health. Team members felt safe to seek help when needed, knowing that they would be met with understanding and compassion.

As they continued to lead their organization with determination and foresight, Wallace and Natasha remained committed to shattering the stigma surrounding mental health and fostering a culture of empathy and support. They knew that by breaking the silence and embracing openness, they could create a workplace where mental health was valued and prioritized, leading to greater resilience and well-being for all.

As Wallace and Natasha delved deeper into their exploration of resilience and stress management, they recognized the importance of promoting work-life integration within their organization. They understood that achieving harmony between work and personal life was essential for maintaining well-being and preventing burnout among their team members.

With unwavering determination, Wallace and Natasha set out to cultivate a culture of work-life integration, where individuals could thrive both professionally and personally.

As they delved into the process, Wallace and Natasha implemented initiatives to promote work-life integration within their organization. They encouraged flexible work arrangements, allowing team members to tailor their schedules to accommodate personal responsibilities and preferences. They also promoted remote work options, recognizing that allowing employees to work from home could enhance work-life balance and productivity.

Armed with this commitment to work-life integration, Wallace and Natasha emphasized the importance of setting boundaries and prioritizing self-care. They encouraged team members to establish clear boundaries between work and personal life, ensuring that they had time to recharge and rejuvenate outside of work hours.

In addition to their efforts to promote work-life integration, Wallace and Natasha led by example, demonstrating the importance of prioritizing their own well-being and personal lives. They shared stories of how they balanced their own professional responsibilities with family time and hobbies, inspiring their team members to prioritize their own work-life harmony.

Through their concerted efforts to promote work-life integration, Wallace and Natasha witnessed positive changes within their organization. Team members felt empowered to prioritize their personal lives without fear of repercussions, leading to greater satisfaction, engagement, and productivity in the workplace.

As they continued to lead their organization with determination and foresight, Wallace and Natasha remained committed to promoting work-life integration as a cornerstone of their leadership philosophy. They knew that by nurturing harmony between work and personal life, they could create a culture where individuals could thrive both inside and outside the workplace, leading to greater resilience and well-being for all.

In their quest for resilience and stress management, Wallace and Natasha encountered numerous trials and challenges that tested their resolve and determination. Yet, they recognized these adversities as opportunities for growth and transformation, believing that resilience was forged in the fires of hardship.

As they delved into the process, Wallace and Natasha embraced the challenges they faced, viewing them as opportunities to cultivate resilience and fortitude within themselves and their team.

Armed with this mindset, Wallace and Natasha navigated each obstacle with grace and determination, drawing upon their inner strength and resilience to overcome adversity. They embraced setbacks as learning opportunities, reframing failures as stepping stones on the path to success.

In addition to their personal growth, Wallace and Natasha fostered a culture of resilience within their organization, encouraging team members to face challenges head-on and learn from their experiences. They provided support and guidance, empowering individuals to navigate adversity with courage and resilience.

Through their concerted efforts to build resilience through adversity, Wallace and Natasha discovered newfound strength and resilience within themselves and their team. They learned that by embracing challenges and setbacks, they could emerge stronger, wiser, and more resilient leaders.

As they continued to lead their organization with determination and foresight, Wallace and Natasha remained committed to cultivating resilience through adversity, knowing that by facing challenges head-on, they could forge a culture of strength and resilience that would withstand the test of time.

# 14

# Chapter Fourteen: Leading Through Crisis

As Wallace and Natasha continued their journey of leadership and resilience, they encountered a defining moment: a crisis that tested their resolve and challenged their ability to lead with courage and compassion.

The crisis came swiftly and unexpectedly, shaking the foundation of their organization and leaving uncertainty in its wake. Yet, amidst the chaos, Wallace and Natasha rose to the occasion, determined to lead their team through the storm with unwavering resolve.

With courage in their hearts and clarity in their minds, Wallace and Natasha rallied their team, providing reassurance and guidance during uncertain times. They communicated openly and transparently, keeping their team informed and empowered to face the challenges ahead.

As they delved into the depths of the crisis, Wallace and Natasha drew upon their resilience and leadership skills, making tough decisions and navigating uncharted waters with grace and determination. They remained calm under pressure, inspiring confidence and unity among their team members.

In addition to leading their team through the crisis, Wallace and Natasha also extended a helping hand to their community, demonstrating their commitment to making a positive impact beyond the walls of their organization. They collaborated with local authorities and organizations, mobilizing resources and support to aid those affected by the crisis.

Through their unwavering leadership and compassion, Wallace and Natasha guided their organization through the storm, emerging stronger and more united than ever before. They learned valuable lessons about resilience, adaptability, and the power of leadership in times of crisis.

As they reflected on their journey, Wallace and Natasha realized that crises were not just challenges to be endured but opportunities for growth and transformation. They emerged from the crisis with a renewed sense of purpose and determination, ready to face whatever challenges lay ahead with courage and resilience.

In the wake of the crisis, Wallace and Natasha recognized the importance of proactive planning and preparation for future challenges. They understood that having a robust crisis management plan in place was essential for navigating tumultuous waters with clarity and confidence.

With a sense of urgency and determination, Wallace and Natasha set out to develop a comprehensive crisis management plan, drawing upon their collective wisdom and experience.

As they delved into the process, Wallace and Natasha engaged their team in brainstorming sessions and strategy meetings, soliciting input and feedback to ensure that the plan was thorough and effective. They identified potential risks and vulnerabilities, mapping out scenarios and response strategies to mitigate the impact of future crises.

Armed with this knowledge, Wallace and Natasha collaborated with key stakeholders to finalize the crisis management plan, outlining clear roles and responsibilities, communication protocols, and escalation procedures. They emphasized the importance of flexibility and adaptability, recognizing that crises were often unpredictable and required agile responses.

In addition to developing the plan itself, Wallace and Natasha invested in training and preparedness exercises to ensure that their team was equipped to execute the plan effectively in times of crisis. They conducted tabletop simulations and role-playing scenarios, providing hands-on experience and building confidence among their team members.

Through their concerted efforts to develop a crisis management plan, Wallace and Natasha instilled a sense of confidence and resilience within their organization. Team members felt empowered and prepared to face future challenges head-on, knowing that they had a roadmap to guide them through the storm.

As they continued to lead their organization with determination and foresight, Wallace and Natasha remained committed to proactive planning and preparation, knowing that by investing in resilience, they could navigate any crisis with grace and confidence.

In the midst of chaos and uncertainty, Wallace and Natasha understood the critical role of effective communication in guiding their organization through the storm. They knew that clear and transparent communication was essential for maintaining trust, calming fears, and providing direction during times of crisis.

With a steady hand and unwavering resolve, Wallace and

## CHAPTER FOURTEEN: LEADING THROUGH CRISIS

Natasha stepped into their roles as communicators-in-chief, determined to navigate the storm with clarity and compassion.

As they delved into the process, Wallace and Natasha crafted a communication strategy that prioritized transparency, empathy, and timeliness. They recognized the importance of keeping their team members informed and engaged, providing regular updates and guidance as the situation evolved.

Armed with this strategy, Wallace and Natasha communicated openly and authentically, addressing concerns and uncertainties with empathy and reassurance. They leveraged various communication channels, including email, virtual town hall meetings, and social media, to reach their team members and stakeholders effectively.

In addition to communicating with their internal audience, Wallace and Natasha also engaged with external stakeholders, including customers, suppliers, and the broader community. They provided regular updates on their organization's response to the crisis, demonstrating their commitment to transparency and accountability.

Through their proactive and empathetic communication efforts, Wallace and Natasha fostered a sense of trust and unity within their organization. Team members felt informed and supported, knowing that their leaders were navigating the storm with clarity and compassion.

As they continued to lead their organization through the crisis, Wallace and Natasha remained committed to effective communication, knowing that by keeping their team members informed and engaged, they could weather any storm with resilience and grace.

In the heat of the crisis, Wallace and Natasha found themselves facing a barrage of urgent decisions that demanded swift action and clear-headedness. They understood that making decisions under pressure was a hallmark of effective leadership, and they rose to the challenge with determination and resolve.

With the weight of responsibility heavy on their shoulders, Wallace and Natasha embraced their roles as decisive leaders, trusting their instincts and relying on their collective wisdom to guide them through the storm.

As they delved into the process, Wallace and Natasha leaned on each other for support, engaging in collaborative decision-making processes that prioritized consensus and alignment. They sought input from key stakeholders, gathering diverse perspectives to inform their decisions and ensure that they were thorough and well-informed.

Armed with this collaborative approach, Wallace and Natasha made tough decisions with confidence and clarity, weighing the risks and benefits carefully before taking decisive action. They understood that in times of crisis, indecision was not an option, and they acted swiftly to address emerging challenges and mitigate potential threats.

In addition to their collaborative decision-making efforts, Wallace and Natasha also trusted their instincts and intuition, recognizing that sometimes, gut feelings could be just as valuable as data and analysis. They remained adaptable and flexible, ready to pivot and course-correct as needed in response to changing circumstances.

Through their decisive leadership in the crucible of crisis, Wallace and Natasha inspired confidence and unity within their organization. Team members looked to them for guidance and direction, knowing that their leaders were making tough decisions with their best interests at heart.

As they continued to navigate the storm with determination

## CHAPTER FOURTEEN: LEADING THROUGH CRISIS

and foresight, Wallace and Natasha remained committed to decisive leadership, knowing that by making tough decisions under pressure, they could steer their organization through any crisis with resilience and grace.

As the tempest raged on, Wallace and Natasha recognized the profound impact of stability and reassurance on their team's morale and well-being. They understood that amidst chaos and uncertainty, providing a sense of stability was essential for maintaining cohesion and resilience within their organization.

With unwavering resolve and empathy, Wallace and Natasha stepped into their roles as anchors of stability, offering reassurance and support to their team members during turbulent times.

As they delved into the process, Wallace and Natasha prioritized frequent and transparent communication, ensuring that their team members were kept informed about the organization's plans and priorities. They provided regular updates on the evolving situation, offering clarity and guidance to alleviate anxiety and uncertainty.

Armed with this commitment to stability, Wallace and Natasha also focused on fostering a culture of trust and psychological safety within their organization. They encouraged open dialogue and vulnerability, creating space for team members to express their concerns and seek support without fear of judgment.

In addition to their communication efforts, Wallace and Natasha led by example, demonstrating resilience and optimism in the face of adversity. They remained calm under pressure, radiating a sense of confidence and determination that inspired their team members to stay strong and resilient.

Through their steadfast leadership and unwavering commitment to stability and reassurance, Wallace and Natasha provided a beacon of hope amidst the storm. Team members looked to them for guidance and support, finding strength and courage in their steady presence.

As they continued to navigate the challenges of the crisis, Wallace and Natasha remained steadfast in their commitment to providing stability and reassurance to their teams, knowing that by anchoring amidst turbulence, they could lead their organization through any storm with resilience and grace.

In the aftermath of the crisis, Wallace and Natasha embarked on a journey of reflection and learning, recognizing the invaluable lessons that could be gleaned from their experiences. They understood that every crisis presented an opportunity for growth and improvement, and they were determined to leverage their experiences to enhance their organization's preparedness for future challenges.

With humility and resolve, Wallace and Natasha delved into a process of post-crisis analysis, examining the events that had unfolded and identifying areas for improvement. They conducted comprehensive debriefs and after-action reviews, soliciting feedback from their team members and stakeholders to gain a comprehensive understanding of what had transpired.

Armed with this knowledge, Wallace and Natasha developed a roadmap for enhancing their organization's preparedness for future crises. They identified gaps in their crisis management plan and communication strategies, implementing corrective actions to address vulnerabilities and improve resilience.

In addition to internal improvements, Wallace and Natasha also sought to foster a culture of continuous learning and improvement within their organization. They encouraged their team members to embrace a growth mindset, viewing

## CHAPTER FOURTEEN: LEADING THROUGH CRISIS

setbacks and failures as opportunities for learning and growth.

Through their concerted efforts to learn from their experiences and improve preparedness, Wallace and Natasha transformed their organization into a more agile and resilient entity. They instilled a sense of confidence and readiness within their team members, knowing that they were better equipped to face future challenges head-on.

As they looked towards the future with optimism and determination, Wallace and Natasha remained committed to the ongoing journey of learning and improvement, knowing that by embracing the lessons of adversity, they could build a stronger and more resilient organization for the challenges that lay ahead.

As the storm of crisis subsided, Wallace and Natasha reflected on the importance of leading with compassion and empathy during difficult times. They understood that while strategy and decisiveness were crucial, it was their ability to connect with their team members on a human level that truly made a difference in times of adversity.

With hearts full of empathy and compassion, Wallace and Natasha embraced their roles as compassionate leaders, committed to supporting and uplifting their team members through the challenges they faced.

Drawing upon their own experiences of vulnerability and uncertainty during the crisis, Wallace and Natasha approached their leadership with a renewed sense of empathy and understanding. They took the time to listen to their team members' concerns and fears, offering a supportive ear and a comforting presence.

In addition to providing emotional support, Wallace and Natasha also sought to alleviate the burdens faced by their team members during difficult times. They implemented flexible work arrangements and mental health support services, recognizing the importance of prioritizing their team members' well-being.

Through their compassionate leadership, Wallace and Natasha fostered a culture of trust and belonging within their organization. Team members felt valued and supported, knowing that their leaders cared deeply about their welfare and happiness.

As they continued to lead with compassion and empathy, Wallace and Natasha inspired their team members to do the same, creating a ripple effect of kindness and support that permeated throughout their organization. They understood that by leading with heart, they could not only weather any storm but also emerge stronger and more united than ever before.

# About the Author

Goodson Mumba is a multifaceted individual known for his diverse expertise and prolific contributions across various fields. As an infopreneur, thought leader, and spiritual leader, he has inspired countless individuals through his insightful teachings and impactful writings. Mumba is also an accomplished author, with several notable works to his name, including "Understanding Corporate Worship," "The Years I Spent in a Week," "Management By Harmony," "The CEO's Diary," "Change to Change" and "Creative Thinking for results" His literary works span topics ranging from business management to personal development and spirituality, reflecting his broad range of interests and insights.

With a Master of Business Leadership (MBL) and a Bachelor of Arts in Theology (BTh), Mumba brings a unique blend of business acumen and spiritual wisdom to his work. His educational background is further enriched by a Group Diploma in Management Studies, providing him with a solid foundation in organizational dynamics and leadership principles. Additionally, Mumba holds diplomas in Education Psychology,

Leadership and Management Styles, Organizational Behaviour, Financial Accounting, Economic Growth and Development, and Project Management, showcasing his commitment to continuous learning and professional development.

Mumba's expertise extends beyond traditional academic disciplines, encompassing areas such as Neuro-Linguistic Programming (NLP) and Positive Psychology. His diverse skill set is complemented by a range of certifications, including Creative Problem Solving and Decision Making, Life Coaching Fundamentals and Techniques, Professional Life Coaching, and Performance Management System Design. These certifications reflect Mumba's dedication to equipping himself with the tools and knowledge necessary to empower others and drive positive change.

As an author, Mumba's writings reflect his deep understanding of human nature, organizational dynamics, and spiritual principles. His works offer practical insights, actionable strategies, and inspirational guidance for individuals seeking personal growth, professional success, and spiritual fulfillment. Mumba's holistic approach to life and leadership resonates with readers worldwide, making him a respected figure in both the business and spiritual communities.

Overall, Goodson Mumba's diverse background, extensive knowledge, and profound insights make him a sought-after speaker, mentor, and author. His commitment to excellence, lifelong learning, and service to others continues to inspire individuals to unlock their full potential and lead lives of purpose and significance.

Goodson Mumba is renowned for initiating the concept of Management by Harmony, revolutionizing traditional management practices with a focus on balanced and holistic approaches. He has authored two influential books on this subject: "Introduction to Management by Harmony" and its sequel, "Management by Harmony."

Mumba's work has significantly impacted the field, offering innovative strategies for fostering organizational harmony and efficiency. His contributions continue to shape contemporary management theories and practices.

www.ingramcontent.com/pod-product-compliance
Lightning Source LLC
Chambersburg PA
CBHW071831210526
45479CB00001B/79